THE MESSAGE GIVEN TO ME BY EXTRA-TERRESTRIALS

They Took Me To Their Planet

By Claude Vorilhon "Raël"

DAVID HILL

THE MESSAGE GIVEN TO ME BY EXTRA-TERRESTRIALS

They Took Me To Their Planet

By Claude Vorilhon "Raël"

Third Printing February, 1989

Published by: AOM Corporation
Puchimondo Ueno 201
1-7-7 Kita-Ueno, Taito-ku
Tokyo, 110 Japan

Printed in Japan

ISBN4-900480-05-3

Translated into English by Raelians from the original two French books whose titles are;

"Le Livre Qui Dit La Vérité" (The Book Which Tells The Truth)

"Les Extra-Terrestres M'ont Emmené Sur Leur Planète" (The Extra-Terrestrials Took Me to Their Planet)

This paper-back version is the second English edition.

The first English edition was printed in Canada, March 1978, as a hard-back, under the title "Space Aliens Took Me To Their Planet".

This paper-back version is slightly different in content from the hard-back version, the difference comes from translation techniques.

Invariably, either style or content are lost during any translation and the translators felt that conveying the author's intended meaning with precision, was more important than literary style.

Furthermore, the French use a different gender system to the English, so wherever it is written "man" or "him" etc. in this book, the meaning obviously includes "woman" or "her" etc. as well.

The Bible translation is based on the King James and the New International version.

CONTENTS

THE BOOK WHICH TELLS THE TRUTH
Chapter I: The Encounter 3
Chapter II: The Truth
Genesis 16
The Flood 25
The Tower of Babel 28
Sodom and Gomorrah 29
The Sacrifice of Abraham 30
Chapter III: The Surveillance of The Chosen Ones
Moses 33
The Trumpets of Jericho 39
Samson The Telepathist 41
The First Residence 44
Elijah The Messenger 46
The Multiplication of Bread 48
The Flying Saucers of Ezekiel 50
The Last Judgement 60
Satan 64
Men Could Not Understand 65
Chapter IV: The Usefulness of Christ
The Conception 72
The Initiation 73
Parallel Humanities 76
Scientific Miracles 80
Deserving the Inheritance 82
Chapter V: The End of the World
1946, Year 1 of the New Era 90
The End of the Church 91

The Creation of the State of Israel 94
The Mistakes of the Church 96
At the Origin of all Religions 98
Man: A Disease of the Universe 100
Evolution: A Myth 103
Chapter VI: The New Commandments
Geniocracy 109
Humanitarianism 111
World Government 115
Your Mission 115
Chapter VII: The Elohim
Atomic Bombs 121
Overpopulation 122
The Secret of Eternity 125
Chemical Education 132
Raelian Movement 134

THE EXTRA-TERRESTRIALS TOOK ME TO THEIR PLANET

Chapter 1: My Life Till The First Encounter
Two Years Already 143
My Childhood, U.F.O. Over Ambert 145
The Pope of The Druids 146
Poetry 148
The Encounter 165
Lectures 169
Chapter 2: The Second Encounter
The Sighting of July 31st, 1975 173
The Second Message 179
Buddhism 185
Neither God nor Soul 189
The Paradise on Earth 193
The Other World 197
Meeting The Ancient Prophets 199
Foretaste of Paradise 210
The New Commandments 218
To The People of Israel 219
Chapter 3: The Keys
Introduction 225
Man 226
Birth 227
Education 228
Sensual Education 232
Fulfilment 235
Society, The Government 243
Meditation and Prayer 250
The Arts 253
Sensual Meditation 254

Human Justice 257
Science 260
The Human Brain 261
The Apocalypse 262
Telepathic Communication 264
The Reward 271
The Guides 282

THE BOOK WHICH TELLS THE TRUTH

THE BOOK WHICH TELLS THE TRUTH

CHAPTER I
THE ENCOUNTER

Ever since the age of nine I have had but one passion: car racing. I created a magazine specialising in this sport three years ago, simply to be able to live in this environment, a sport where man is always trying to surpass himself, while trying to surpass others. Since my early childhood I dreamed of one day being a race-car driver and following in the footsteps of someone as famous as Fangio. Thanks to contacts made through the magazine I founded, I was given an opportunity to race. About ten trophies are now adorning my apartment resulting from these opportunities.

On December 13th 1973, I went to the volcanoes overlooking Clermont-Ferrand (France). It was more to get a breath of fresh air than to take a drive in my car. My legs were itching after a full year of following the races from circuit to circuit, almost always living on four wheels, so to speak.

The air was cool at the time, and the sky rather grey with a background mist. I walked and jogged a little, and left the path where my car was parked, aiming to reach the center of the crater called Puy-de-Lassolas where I often came in the summertime for picnics with my family. What a superb and breath-taking place it was. To think that thousands of years ago, where my feet were touching, lava was erupting at incredibly high temperatures. Decorative volcanic "bombs" can still be found in the remains. The stunted vegetation resembled that of Provence (France) without sunshine. I was about to leave and I looked once again at the top of the circular mountain, made by an accumulation of slag, remembering how many times I had slid down those steep slopes as if I were on skis. Suddenly, in the fog, I saw a red light flashing, then a sort of helicopter coming down towards me. A helicopter, however, makes a noise, and I heard absolutely nothing, not even the slightest whistling. A balloon maybe? The object was about 20 metres above the ground, and I could see it had a flattened shape. A flying saucer!

I had always firmly believed in their existence, but I never dreamed I would actually see one. It measured about seven metres in diameter, two and one half metres in height, and was flat underneath and conicular on top. At the bottom flashed a very bright red light, and at the top a white light like that of a photo flash cube, flashed intermittently. The white light was so intense that I could not look at it without blinking. The object continued to descend, without the slightest noise, and immobilised itself at about two metres above the ground. I was petrified and stayed absolutely still. I was not afraid, but rather filled with joy to be living such a great moment. I bitterly regretted not having brought along my camera. Then, the incredible happened: a trap-door opened beneath the machine, and a kind of stairway was lowered to the ground. I realised that a being was about to appear, and I wondered what it was going to look like.

First appeared two feet, then two legs, and I was reassured a little, for it seemed I was about to meet a man. What I had at first thought to be a child, descended the stairway and then walked straight towards me. I could see it was certainly not a child, even if it measured only about 1.2 metres in height. His eyes were slightly almond-shaped, the hair was black and long, and he had a small black beard. I still had not moved, and he stopped about 10 metres from me. He wore a sort of green flying suit, or overalls, which appeared to be made of only one piece of material, and though his head seemed to be exposed, I could see a strange sort of halo around him. Not really a halo, but the air surrounding his face was brilliant and seemed to vibrate, or shimmer. It looked like an invisible shield, like a bubble, so fine that you could barely see it. His skin was white with a slightly greenish tinge, something like that of a human suffering from liver trouble. He smiled slighly and I thought it best to return his smile. I felt rather ill at ease, so I smiled and bowed my head slighly as if to say hello.

He answered with the same sign. I had to find out if he could hear me, so I asked, "Where do you come from?"

He answered in a strong and very articulate voice, which sounded a little nasal to me, "From very far away."

"Do you speak French?"

"I speak all the languages of the earth."

"Do you come from another planet?"

"Yes," he replied.

As he talked he moved within two metres of me.

"Is it the first time you have visited the earth?"

"Oh no!"

"Do you come often?"

"Very often is the least I could say."

"Why did you come here?"

"Today, to talk to you."

"To me?"

"Yes, to you Claude Vorilhon, editor of a small sports-car magazine, married, and father of two children."

"How do you know all this?"

"We have been watching you for a long time."

"Why me?"

"This is exactly what I want to tell you. Why have you come here on this cold winter morning?"

"I don't know, ... I felt like walking in the fresh air ...."

"Do you come here often?"

"In the summer yes, but practically never in this season."

"So why today? Had you planned this walk for a long time?"

"No. I don't really know. When I awoke this morning I suddenly felt an urge to come here."

"You came because I wanted to see you. Do you believe in telepathy?"

"Yes, of course, it is a subject which I have always been interested in as well as what we humans call 'flying saucers', but I never thought of seeing one personally."

"So then, I have used telepathy to get you to come here because I have many things to tell you.

Have you read the Bible?"

"Yes, but why do you ask?"

"Have you been reading it for a long time?"

"No, as a matter of fact I bought it only a few days ago."

"Why?"

"I really don't know, but suddenly I had an urge to read it...."

"Again I used telepathy to make you decide to buy it. I have chosen you for a very difficult mission, and I have many things to tell you, so come into my machine where we can talk more comfortably."

I followed him, climbing the small staircase located beneath the machine. As I looked at it more closely, I observed that the flying object resembled a flattened bell with a full and bulging bottom. Inside were two seats facing each other, and the temperature was mild even though the door was still open. There was no lamp, but a natural light which came from all sides. There were no instruments like those of an aircraft cockpit. The floor was made of a sparking alloy which was slightly bluish. The seat on which I sat was the larger, but also the lowest to the floor, so that the little man sitting in front of me in a colourless, slightly transparent, but very comfortable chair, would have his face at the same level as mine.

He touched a spot on the wall and the whole machine became transparent, except for its top and bottom. It felt like being in the open air, but at a mild temperature. He invited me to take off my coat, which I did, and then he started to speak.

"You regret not having brought along your camera so that you could have talked about our meeting to the whole world, and with proof in your hands?"

"Yes, of course...."

"Listen to me. You will tell humans the truth about what they are, and what we are. Judging from their reactions, we will be able to know if we can show ourselves freely and officially. Wait until you know everything before you start speaking, so that you can defend yourself properly against those people who will not believe you and bring them incontestable proof. You will write down everything I will tell you and you will publish the writings in book form."

"But why did you choose me?"

"For many reasons. First of all, we need someone who lives in a country where new ideas are welcomed and where it is possible to talk about such ideas openly. Democracy was born in France, and this country has a reputation the world over of being the country of freedom. Also, we needed someone who is intelligent and quite open to everything. Above all we needed someone who is a freethinker without being anti-religious. Because you were born of a Jewish father and a Catholic mother, we considered you as an ideal link between two very important peoples in the history of the world. Besides, your activity does not predispose you at all to making incredible revelations, thus making your words more believable. Not being a scientist, you will not complicate things, but will explain them simply. Since you are not a literary man, you will not compose complicated sentences difficult to read for a great many people. We finally decided to choose someone who was born after the first atomic explosion in 1945, and you were born in 1946. We have in fact been following you since your birth, and even before. This is why we have chosen you. Now, do you have any other question?"

"Where do you come from?"

"From a far distant planet of which I will tell you nothing for fear that men of the earth would be unwise and disturb our tranquillity."

"Is your planet very far away?"

"Very far. When I tell you the distance you will understand that it is impossible to reach it with your present scientific and technical knowledge."

"What are you called?"

"We are men like you, and we live on a planet similar to the earth."

"How long does it take you to come to earth?"

"As long as it takes to think about it."

"Why do you come to earth?"

"To observe the evolution of humans and to watch over them. They are the future, we are the past."

"Are there many people on your planet?"

"There are more people than on yours."

"I would like to visit your planet. Would it be possible?"

"No. First of all, you could not live there because the atmosphere is different from yours, and

DRAWINGS OF THE FLYING SAUCER

A) In the sky:

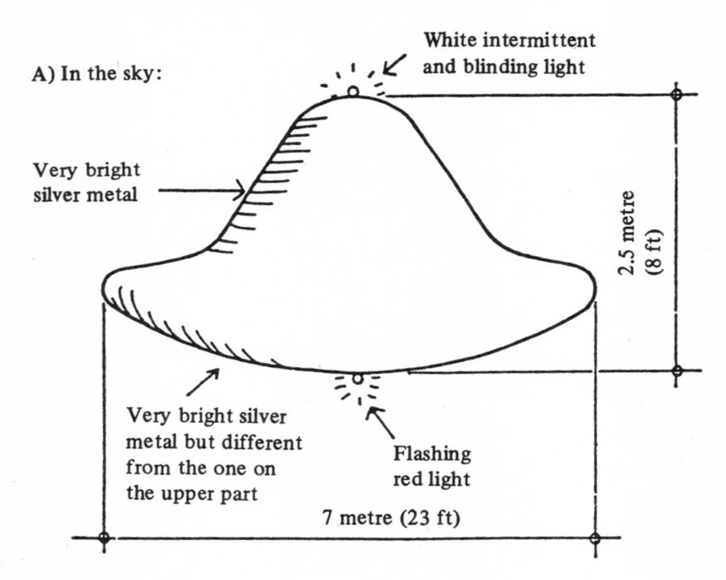

B) When the man came out:

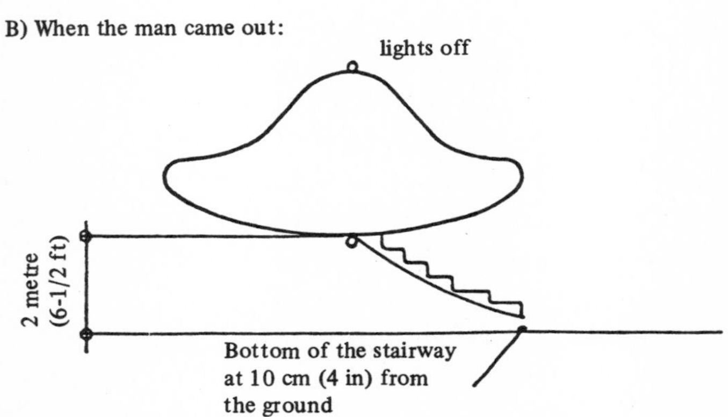

CROSS SECTION OF THE FLYING SAUCER

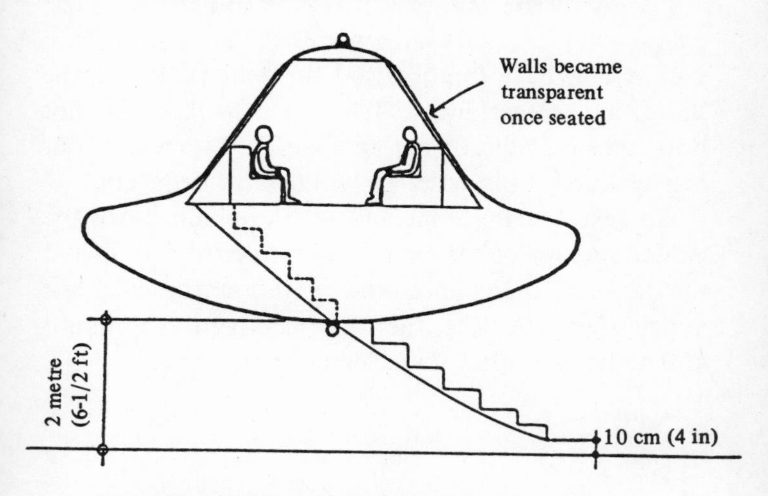

EMBLEM ENGRAVED ON THE FLYING SAUCER
AND ON THE MAN'S SUIT

- On the side of the flying saucer: 10 cm (4 in) high
- On the man's suit: 3 cm (1-1/5 in) high

Meaning: That which is above is like that which is below and everything is cyclic.

you are not trained for such a journey."

"But why meet here?"

"Because the crater of a volcano is an ideal place, away from irksome people. I shall now leave you. Come back tomorrow at the same time with the Bible, and something to take notes with. Do not bring any metallic object and speak to no one of our conversation; otherwise, we will never meet again."

He gave me my coat and let me climb down the ladder and waved his hand. The ladder folded up and the door closed and, still without the slightest murmur or whistling, the craft rose gently, to about 400 metres and then disappeared in the mist.

CHAPTER II
THE TRUTH

Genesis
The Flood
The Tower of Babel
Sodom and Gomorrah
The Sacrifice of Abraham

Genesis

The following day I was at the meeting place with a notebook, a pen, and the Bible. The machine reappeared on time, and I found myself again facing the same little man, who invited me to enter and sit in the comfortable chair. I had spoken to no one about this, not even to my closest friends, and he was happy to learn that I had remained discreet. He suggested I should take notes and started to speak.

"A very long time ago, on our distant planet, men had reached a level of technical and scientific knowledge comparable to the one you will soon reach. They started by creating primitive and embryonic forms of life, living cells in test tubes. Everyone was thrilled, and they perfected their techniques and created bizarre little animals. The government, under pressure from public opinion, ordered the scientists to stop their experiments for fear they would create monsters, which would become dangerous to our society. In fact, one of these animals broke loose and killed several people. Since inter-planetary and intergalactic explorations has progressed simultaneously, they decided to set out for a distant planet where they could find nearly all the necessary conditions to pursue their experiments. They chose the earth where you live. At this point I ask you to take the Bible where you will find traces of the truth, traces which of course have been slighly distorted by transcribers who could not conceive of such highly technical things, and could therefore only attribute what was described to a mystical and supernatural force."

"Only the parts of the Bible that I will translate are important. The others are only poetical babblings of which I will not talk. You can surely appreciate that, thanks to the law which said that the Bible had to be recopied without changing the smallest sign, the profound meaning was kept intact, even if the text was loaded with mystical and futile sentences throughout the millenniums."

"Let us start with Genesis, Chapter 1: 'In the beginning Elohim created the heavens and the earth.' Genesis 1:1.

Elohim, unjustly translated in some Bibles by the word God, means in Hebrew 'those who came from the sky' and furthermore, the word is plural. It means that the scientists from our world searched for a suitable planet to fully realise their projects. They 'created', or rather 'discovered' the earth, and realised it contained all of the necessary elements for the creation of artificial life, even if its atmosphere was not quite the same as theirs.

'And the spirit of Elohim moved across the waters.' Genesis 1:2.

They made reconnaissance flights and what you might call artificial satellites were placed around the earth to study its constitution and atmosphere. The earth at that time was entirely covered with water and thick fog. 'Elohim saw that the light was good.' Genesis 1:4.

To create life on Earth, it was important to know whether the sun was sending harmful rays to the Earth's surface and this question was studied.

It turned out that the Sun was heating the earth correctly without sending out harmful rays. The 'light was good'.

'There was a night and there was a morning the first day.' Genesis 1:5.

These studies took quite some time. The 'day' corresponds to the period during which your Sun rises under the same sign on the day of the vernal equinox, in other words, two thousand terrestrial years approximately.

'He divided the waters under the heavens from the waters above the firmament.' Genesis 1:7.

After studying the cosmic rays above the clouds, they descended below them but stayed above the waters, that is to say, between waters above the firmament, i.e., the clouds and the waters below, i.e. the ocean covering the whole planet.

'Let the waters under the heavens be gathered together into one place and let dry land appear.' Genesis 1:9.

After they had studied the surface of the ocean, they studied its bottom and determined that it was not very deep and also fairly even everywhere. So then, with fairly strong explosions, acting rather like bulldozers, they raised matter from the bottom of the seas and piled it into one place to form a continent. Originally there was on earth only one continent and your scientists have recently acknowledged that all the continents which had drifted apart over many years, fitted perfectly one into the other to form only one.

'Let the earth grow vegetation, grass and trees.... which have in them their own seed according to their species.' Genesis 1:11.

On this magnificent and gigantic laboratory they created vegetable cells from nothing other than chemicals which produced various types of plants. All their efforts were aimed at reproduction. The few blades of grass they had created had to reproduce on their own. They scattered on this immense continent in small scientific research teams, and everyone according to his inspiration and the climate, created different varieties of plants. They met at regular intervals to compare their research, and their creations. The people from their own planet followed their progress from afar with passion and amazement. The most brilliant of the artists came and joined the scientists so as to give some plants a purely decorative and agreeable role, either by their appearance or by their perfume.

'Let there be lights in the heavens to separate the day from the night, and let them be used as signs for the seasons, for the days and for the years.' Genesis 1:14.

They could measure by observing the stars and the sun, the duration of the days, the months, and the years on earth, which was going to help them regulate their life on this new planet so different from theirs, where the days and the years did not have the same duration. Research in astronomy enabled them to situate themselves perfectly and to know the earth better.

'Let the waters teem with an abundance of living animals, and let the birds fly above the earth.' Genesis 1:20.

Then, they created the first aquatic animals from plankton to small fish, then very large fish. They also created seaweed to balance this little world, so that the little fish could eat and the bigger fish could eat them in return, etc., so that a natural balance would be established, and that one species did not entirely destroy another species to feed themselves. This is what you now refer to as ecology. They were successful. They met often and organised contests to determine which team of scientists had created the most beautiful or most interesting animals.

After the fish they created the birds, under pressure from the artists it must be said, who went out of their way to create the craziest colours and the most stunning forms of animals, some of which had trouble flying because of their cumbersome but beautiful feathers. The contests went even further, to include not only the physical characteristics but the behaviour of these animals, including the wonderful dances of the mating rituals. Some other groups of scientists, on the other hand, created frightful animals, indeed monsters, which proved those people who had opposed the creation plans on their own planet to be right. There were dragons, or what have been called Dinosaurus or Brontosaurus, etc.

'Let the living animals emerge from the earth

according to their species: livestock, reptiles, wild animals, according to their species.' Genesis 1:24.

After the sea and the air, they created terrestrial animals on a planet where the vegetation had by then become magnificent. There was food for the herbivores. These were the first land animals which had been created. Later they created some carnivores so as to balance the herbivore population. In this case too, the species had to maintain equilibrium. Those men came from the planet I come from. I am one of those people who created life on earth.

It was at that moment that the most skilful amongst us wished to create an artificial man like us. Each team set to work, and very soon we were able to compare our creations. But the planet where we came from was outraged when they heard that we were making "test tube children" who could come and threaten their world. They feared that the new humans could become a danger if their mental capacities or powers would turn out to be superior to that of their creators. We had to let them live in a very primitive way, without letting them know anything scientific, and while mystifying our actions. The number of teams of creators is easy to work out. Each human race corresponds to a team of creators.

'Let us make man in our image after our likeness: Let them have authority on the fish of the sea and the birds of the sky, on the livestock, on all the wild animals and on áll the reptiles which crawl on the earth.' Genesis 1:26.

In our image. You can see that the resemblance

is striking. That is when the problems started for us. The team located in the country known today as Israel, which at that time was not far from Greece and Turkey on the original continent, was comprised of brilliant creators, perhaps 'the' most brilliant team. Their animals were the most beautiful, and their plants had the sweetest perfumes. It is that which you call the earthly paradise. The humans they created were the most intelligent. So they had to take steps to ensure that the created did not surpass the creator. He had to be confined in ignorance of the great scientific secrets while being educated to be able to measure his intelligence. 'Of every tree in the garden you may eat, but of the tree of knowledge of good and evil you shall not eat of it, for on the day that you eat of it, you shall die.' Genesis 2:17.

This means: you can learn all you want, read all of the books that we have here at your disposal, but never touch the scientific books, otherwise you will die.

'He brought to man all the animals to see what he would call them.' Genesis 2:19.

Man had to know very well the plants and the animals living around him, their way of life, and the way to get food from them. The creators taught him the names and the powers of everything that existed around him, for botany and zoology were not considered dangerous for him. Imagine the joy of this team of scientists, having two children, a male and a female, running around, and to whom they were quite eagerly teaching all kinds of things.

'The serpent...said to the woman...of the fruit of the tree which is in the midst of the garden...you would not die, for Elohim knows that on the day you eat thereof, your eyes will be opened and you shall be as Gods.' Genesis 3:1-5.

Amongst all of the scientists in this team, some felt a deep love for their little humans, their 'creations,' and they wanted to give these children a complete education so as to make them scientists like themselves. They told these young adults that they could pursue their scientific studies and in so doing they would become as knowledgeable as their creators.

'Then the eyes of them both were opened and they knew that they were naked.' Genesis 3:7.

Then they understood that they also could become creators in return, and became angry at their fathers for having kept them away from the scientific books, comparing them to the dangerous animals kept in their laboratories.

"Yahwe (Elohim) said to the serpent: be damned... on your belly you shall crawl, and dust you shall eat all the days of your life.' Genesis 3:14.

The 'serpent' this small group of creators who had wished to tell the truth to 'Adam and Eve', were condemned by the government of the original planet to live in exile on earth, while the other creators had to put a stop to their experiments and to leave the earth. 'Elohim made for the man and his wife coats of skin and clothed them.' Genesis 3:21.

The creators gave them primitive means to ensure

their survival, enough to manage without any contacts with them. The Bible has preserved a sentence which is very close to the original document.

'Now the man has become as one of us, thanks to science.... Now we must ensure that he does not put out his hand to take from the tree of life, eat, and live forever.' Genesis 3:22.

Human life is very short, but there exists a scientific way to prolong it. A scientist who studies all of his life starts making discoveries when he becomes old, and this is the reason why the progress of humanity is so slow. If humans could live ten times longer, scientific knowledge would take a giant leap. If at the start they could have lived much longer, they would have become our equals quite rapidly, because their mental faculties are slightly superior to ours. They are unaware of their potentials. As I mentioned before, more specifically, the people of Israel had been selected in a contest as the type of humanoid on earth to be the most successful due to their intelligence and their genius. This would explain why they have always been considered to be the 'chosen people'. It is true, they were the people chosen by the teams of creators gathered together to judge their works. You can see for yourself the number of geniuses born out of that race.

'So he drove out man and placed at the East of the garden of Eden the Cherubim and a flaming sword which turned every way to guard the way to the tree of life.' Genesis 3:24.

Soldiers with atomic disintegrating weapons were

placed at the entrance to the creator's residence to prevent humans from stealing more scientific knowledge.

The Flood

Let us move to Genesis Chapter 4: 'And in process of time it came to pass that Cain brought of the fruit of the ground to Yahwe, and Abel also brought of the firstlings of his flock.' Genesis 4:3.

The creators in exile who were left under military surveillance urged humans to bring them food, so as to show their superiors that the newly created men were good, and that they would never turn against their fathers. They managed to obtain permission for the leaders of these first humans to benefit from the 'tree of life', and this explains how they lived for so many years. Adam nine hundred and thirty years, Seth nine hundred and twelve years, Enosh nine hundred and five years, etc.

'When men began to multiply on the face of the earth, and daughters were born unto them, the sons of Elohim saw that the daughters of men were beautiful. They took them as wives of all they had chosen.' Genesis 6:1-2.

The creators living in exile took the most beautiful daughters of men and made them their wives.

'My spirit shall not always stay with man for he also is flesh, yet his days shall be one hundred and twenty years.' Genesis 6:3.

Longevity is not hereditary, and the children of the

new humans did not automatically benefit from 'the 'tree of life', much to the relief of the authorities of the distant planet. And so the secret was lost, and mankind's progress was slowed down.

'When the sons of Elohim came in unto the daughtters of men and had children by them, they were the heroes of old, men of renown.' Genesis 6:4.

There you have the proof that the creators could have intercourse with the daughters of the men they had created in their image, so as to have exceptional children. These actions seemed very dangerous to the distant planet. The scientific progress on earth was fantastic, and so they decided to destroy their creation.

'And Yahwe saw that man had done much evil on earth, and that his thoughts and inclinations were always evil.' Genesis 6:5.

The evil was the desire of people to become equal to their creators as scientific and independent people. Good for them would have been to keep humans as primitives, vegetating on the earth. Their evil was their will to progress, enabling them one day to overtake their creators. They then decided from their distant planet, to destroy all life on earth by sending nuclear missiles. However, the exiled creators, informed of the project, asked Noah to build a spaceship which would orbit the earth during the cataclysm, and contain a couple of each species to be preserved, figuratively speaking. In reality, and your scientific knowledge will very soon enable you to understand, a single living cell of each species, male and female, is all that is necessary to create the whole being. Something like the first living cell of a being in the womb of its mother which already possesses all the information to create a human, even to the colour of the eyes and hair.

This was a colossal task, but it was completed on time. When the explosion took place, life was preserved a few thousand kilometres above the earth. The continent was submerged by a gigantic tidal wave which destroyed all forms of life on its surface.

'The ark was lifted above the earth.' Genesis 7:17.

As you can clearly see, it is said that the ark was lifted 'above' the earth and not 'on' the water. Then they had to wait until there was not more dangerous radioactive fallout.

'The waters grew above the earth during one hundred and fifty days.' Genesis 7:24.

The spacecraft, with its three stories ('you shall build it in stages, the lower, the second and the third') landed on earth. Besides Noah, it carried a couple of each human race of the earth.

'Elohim remembered Noah...a wind blew across the earth and the waters became still.' Genesis 8:1.

After having monitored the level of radioactivity and dispersed it scientifically, the creators told Noah to let the animals out to see if they could survive in this atmosphere, and the operation was successful. They survived in the open air. The creators asked the human survivors to work and multiply, while showing their gratitude to their benefactors who had created, them and saved them from destruction. Noah agreed to give a portion of all the harvest to the creators to ensure their survival.

'Noah built an altar for Yahwe, he took all the pure beasts and all the pure birds, and he made an offering on the altar.' Genesis 8:20.

The creators were happy to see that the humans looked after them and they promised never to destroy the creation again. They understood that it was only normal for them to want to progress.

'Every inclination of man's heart is evil.' Genesis 8:21.

Man's objective is scientific progress. Each human race was replaced in its original place of creation, and all the animals were recreated from the cells which had been preserved aboard the ark.

'From them came the separated nations on earth after the flood.' Genesis 10:32.

The Tower of Babel

But the most intelligent race, the people of Israel, were making remarkable progress and soon undertook the conquest of space with the help of the exiled creators. The latter wanted humans to go to the creator's planet to obtain their pardon, by showing that humans were as intelligent and scientifically evolved, just as they were grateful and peaceful. So they built an enormous rocket: The Tower of Babel.

'And now they have decided to do this, henceforward nothing they plan to do will be beyond their reach.' Genesis 11:6.

The people on our planet became frightened when they heard about this. They were still observing the earth and knew that life had not been destroyed.

'Let us go down there and confuse their speech, so that they will not understand what they say to one another.' 'So Yahwe scattered them from there over all the earth.' Genesis 11:17.

They came and took the Jews who had the most advanced scientific knowledge and scattered them all over the continent, among primitive tribes, in countries where nobody could understand them because the language was different, and they destroyed all of their scientific instruments.

Sodom and Gomorrah

The exiled creators were pardoned and allowed to return to their original planet, where they pleaded the case of their magnificent creation. In turn, the whole distant planet fixed their eyes on the earth, because it was inhabited by creatures that they had created. But among the humans who had been dispersed a few felt a desire for vengeance, so they gathered in the towns of Sodom and Gomorrah and, having managed to salvage a few scientific secrets, they prepared an expedition aimed at punishing those who had tried to destroy them. The creators sent two spies to investigate what was going on.

'And there came two angels to Sodom in the evening ....' Genesis 19:1.

Men tried to kill them, but the spies managed to blind them with a pocket atomic weapon.

'And they smote them with blindness, both small and great.' Genesis 19:11.

They warned the men who were peaceful to leave town, because they were going to destroy it with an atomic explosion.

'Leave this place: for Yahwe is going to destroy the city.' Genesis 19:14.

As the people were leaving the town, they were in no particular hurry, not realising what an atomic explosion could mean.

'Flee for your lives; do not look back and do not stop anywhere.' Genesis 19:17.

And the bomb fell on Sodom and Gomorrah.

'Then Yahwe rained down fire and brimstone from the skies on Sodom and Gomorrah. He overthrew those cities and destroyed all the plain, and all inhabitants of the cities, and that which grew upon the ground. But Lot's wife looked back and she became a pillar of salt.' Genesis 19:24-26.

As you now know, the burns caused by an atomic explosion killed those who were too near and made them appear like a salt statue.

The Sacrifice of Abraham

Later, the creators wished to see if the people of Israel, and particularly their leader, still had positive feelings towards them, even in the semi-primitive state into which they had relapsed, the majority of the 'brains' having been destroyed. That is what is related in the paragraph in which Abraham wants to sacrifice his own son. The creators tested him to see if his feelings toward them were sufficiently strong. The experiment was fortunately conclusive.

'Do not raise your hand against the boy; do not touch him. Now I know that you fear Elohim.' Genesis 22:12.

There you have it. Assimilate and write down everything I have just told you. I will tell you more about it tomorrow."

Once again the little man took leave of me, and the spaceship rose slowly. Because the sky was clearer this time, I was able to watch its take-off in greater detail. It immobilised at about 400 metres, then, still without the slightest noise, the vessel turned red as if it was heating up, then white as a white hot metal, then a sort of bluish-purple like an enormous spark which was impossible to look at. Then it completely disappeared.

CHAPTER III
THE SURVEILLANCE OF THE CHOSEN ONES

Moses

The Trumpets of Jericho

Samson The Telepathist

The First Residence

Elijah The Messenger

The Multiplication of Bread

The Flying Saucers of Ezekiel

The Last Judgement

Satan

Men Could Not Understand

Moses

The next day I again met with my visitor and he continued his story.

"In Genesis 28 there is another description of our presence:

'A ladder which rested on the ground with its top reaching to heaven, and the angels of Elohim were going up and down upon it.' Genesis 28:12.

But humans, having relapsed into a primitive state after the most intelligent among them were destroyed, as well as the centres of progress like Sodom and Gomorrah, began, rather stupidly, to adore pieces of stone and idols, forgetting those who had created them.

'Put away the strange gods that are among you.' Genesis 35:2.

In Exodus we appear before Moses:

'And the angel of Yahwe appeared unto him in a flame of fire out of the midst of a bush, behold, the bush burned with fire, and the bush was not consumed.' Exodus 3:2.

A rocket landed in front of him, and the description of it corresponds to that which a Brazilian tribesman would make today if we were to land before him in a flying vessel, where the bright light would appear among the trees without burning them. The people chosen as the most intelligent had lost their most brilliant minds, and had become the slaves of the neighbouring tribesmen who were far greater in number because they had not undergone the same destruction. It was necessary to return this people's dignity by returning their land to them.

The beginning of Exodus describes all that we had to do to help liberate the people of Israel. When they departed we guided them to the country which we had destined for them.

'And Yahwe went before them by day in a pillar of a cloud, to lead them the way, and by night in a pillar of fire, to give them light, to go by day and night.' Exodus 13:21.

In order to slow down the march of the Egyptians who had started to pursue them:

'The pillar of the cloud went from before their face and stood behind them...and it was a cloud and darkness to one side, but it gave light by night to the other' Exodus 14: 19-20.

The smoke emitted behind the people of Israel made a curtain which slowed down the pursuants.

Then the crossing of the water was made possible by a repulsion beam which cleared a passage.

'And make the sea dry land, and the waters divided.' Exodus 14:21.

'Thus Yahwe saved Israel.' Exodus 14:30.

While they were crossing the desert, the chosen people suffered from hunger:

'Upon the face of the wilderness fine flakes appeared, fine as hoarfrost on the ground.' Exodus 16:14.

The manna was nothing more than a chemical food made of pulverized synthetics, which when laid on earth's surface, swelled with the early morning dew.

As for the staff of Moses which allowed him 'to draw water from the rock' (Exodus 17:16), it was nothing but a detector of underground aquatic pools, similar to those which you presently use to find oil for example. Once the water is located one only has to dig.

Then a certain number of rules are expressed in Chapter 20 of Exodus. Because the Israelites were so primitive, they needed laws regarding morals and especially hygiene. These were outlined in the commandments. The creators came to dictate these laws to Moses on Mount Sinai, and they arrived in a flying vessel:

'There were thunders and lightnings, and a thick cloud upon the Mount, and the voice of the trumpet exceedingly long.' Exodus 19:16.

'And Mount Sinai was altogether in smoke because Yahwe descended upon it in fire: and the smoke thereof ascended as the smoke of a furnace, and the whole Mount quaked greatly. And the voice of the trumpet sounded long and waxed louder and louder.' Exodus 19: 18-19.

But the creators were afraid of being invaded or mistreated by humans. It was essential that they be respected, even venerated, so that they would be in no danger.

'The people cannot come up Mount Sinai...but let not the priests and the people break through to come unto Yahwe for fear that he may break out against them.' Exodus 19: 23-24.

'And Moses alone shall come near Yahwe: but the elders of Israel and the people may not go up with him at all.' Exodus 24:2.

'They saw the God of Israel: under his feet there was as it were, a pavement of sapphire, clear blue as the very heavens.' Exodus 24:10.

There you have a description of the pedestal upon which one of the creators presented himself, and it was made of the same bluish alloy as the floor of the machine on which we are now standing.

'And the sight of the glory of Yahwe was like devouring fire on the top of the Mount.' Exodus 24:17.

There you have a description of the 'Glory', the flying vessel in reality and, as you have already noticed, upon take off it has a colouration similar to fire.

This team of creators was going to live on earth for some time, and they wished to eat fresh food: that is why they asked the Israelities to bring them provisions regularly, also riches which they wanted to take back to their own planet. I suppose you might call it colonisation.

'You shall accept whatever contribution each man shall freely offer. This is what you shall accept: gold, silver, copper, violet, purple and scarlet yard; etc....' Exodus 25: 3-4.

They also decided that they would like to live more comfortably, so they asked the humans to build them a residence according to plans they had drawn up. The plans are described in Chapter 26 of the Book of

Exodus. In this residence they would meet the representatives of the people: it was a meeting-place where men brought food and gifts as a pledge of submission.

'He entered the tent of the meeting-place.' Exodus 33:8.

'When Moses entered it, the pillar of cloud came down and stayed at the entrance to the tent while Yahwe spoke with Moses.' Exodus 33:9.

'And Yahwe would speak with Moses face to face, as one man speaks to another.' Exodus 33:11.

Just like today, I can speak to you and you can speak to me, man to man.

'My face you cannot see, for no mortal man may see me and live.' Exodus 33:20.

There you have reference to the difference in atmosphere between our planets. A man is unable to see his creators unless the latter are protected by a pressurised suit, because the terrestrial atmosphere is not appropriate to them. If man came to our planet, he would see the creators without a space suit, but he would die, because the atmosphere is not suitable for him. The entire beginning of the Leviticus explains how the foods offered to the creators should be brought for their provisions. For example, in Leviticus 21:17:

'No man among your descendants for all time who has any physical defect shall come to present the food to his God.'

This is obviously to avoid that any sick or deformed men, symbols of failure and unbearable to the eyes of the creators, present themselves before them.

In the book of Numbers, 11:17, there is a very exact description of the manna which your chemists could very easily reproduce.

'And the manna was as coriander seed, and the colour thereof as the colour of bdellium...the taste of it was as the taste of fresh oil.'

But this manna was nothing more than a chemical food to which the creators preferred fresh fruits and vegetables.

'They will bring unto Yahwe the first-ripe fruits of all produce in their land.'

Further, the creators taught men how to inject themselves to treat snake bites.

'Make a fiery serpent and set it upon a pole so that anyone who had been bitten could look at it and live.'

As soon as someone was bitten he 'looked' at the 'serpent of brass', i.e. a syringe was brought to him with which he was injected with serum.

Finally the journey which led the 'chosen people' to the 'promised land' came to an end. Following the advice of the creators they destroyed the idols of the local primitive peoples and took over their territories.

'You will destroy all their melted metal statues and you will possess the country.'

The chosen people finally reached their promised land:

'Because he loved your fathers he has chosen their race after them.'

In Joshua 3:15, we read about the crossing of Jordan:

'When the priests carrying the Ark reached the Jordan...the water coming down from upstream was brought to a standstill. It piled up like a bank for a long way back...the waters were completely cut off and the people crossed over opposite Jericho'.

The creators helped the 'chosen people' pass without getting their feet wet, just as they had done in their escape from the Egyptians, by using the same repellent ray.

The Trumpets of Jericho

At the end of Chapter 5 in the book of Joshua, there is a contact between a military creator and the chosen people regarding the resistance of the City of Jericho.

'I am here as captain of the army of Yahwe.' Joshua 5:14.

A military counsellor was sent to the Jewish people to assist them in the siege of Jericho. You will easily understand how the walls were knocked down. You know that a very high voice of a singer can easily crack a crystal glass. By using highly amplified supersonic waves, one can knock down a brick wall. This is what was done, with the help of a very complicated instrument which the Bible calls a 'trumpet'.

'when they make a long blast with the ram's horn, and when you hear the sound of the trumpet.....the wall of the city shall fall down flat' Joshua 6:5.

At a given moment the supersonic waves are emitted in a synchronised way and the walls fell down.

A little later on a real bombardment takes place:

'Yahwe hurled great hailstones at them out of the sky and more died from the hailstones than the Israelites slew by the sword.' Joshua 10:11.

'A full scale bombardment which killed more people than the steel arms of the Israelites.'

One of the most misunderstood passages is in Joshua 10 where is stated:

'And the sun stood, and the moon stayed, until the people had avenged themselves upon their enemies.'

Which simply means that the war was a flash war, which lasted one day (it is mentioned later that the war lasted 'nearly a whole day') and was so short, considering the extent of land conquered, that men thought the sun had stood still.

In the Book of Judges 6, one of the creators is again in contact with a man called Gideon who continues to supply him with food.

'The angel of Yahwe put forth the end of the staff that was in his hand, and touched the flesh and the unleavened cakes: and there rose up fire out of the rock and consumed the flesh and the unleavened cakes. Then the angel of Yahwe departed out of his sight.' Judges 6:21.

With the help of a scientific method, the creators, who are unable to 'eat' in the open air because of their pressurised suits, could, in case of need, serve themselves 'offerings' by extracting the essentials from a flexible tube, a 'cane', capable of feeding them. This process radiates flames, which made people of the era think 'sacrifices to God' were being made.

In Chapter 7 of the Book of Judges, three hundred men with 'trumpets' surrounded the enemy camp, and, using amplified supersonic instruments, they all blew together so as to drive all the people mad. You now know that certain high-pitched sounds carried to extremes, could drive anyone mad. Indeed the surrounded soldiers went wild, fought among themselves, and ran away.

Samson The Telepathist

In Judges 13, there is yet another example of the mating between the creators and human women.

'And the angel of Yahwe appeared unto the woman and said: you are barren and have no child, but you shall conceive and give birth to a son.'

It was necessary that the fruit of this union be healthy so that the behaviour of the child could be studied. This is why he tells her, 'And drink not wine nor strong drink, and eat not any unclear thing, for lo thou shalt conceive and bear a son.'

'And no razor shall come on his head, for the child shall be a Nazarite unto God from the womb'.

'And the angel of Elohim came again to the woman who was sitting in the fields; her husband was not with her.'

You can easily imagine what happened during the husband's absence...it was an easy task for the scientists to cure her sterility, in order to make her well aware that she was going to give birth to quite an exceptional being, and that she should take the utmost care of it. It was magnificent for the creators to mate with a daughter of men. This permitted them to have sons ruling directly on the earth, in this atmosphere which was not fitted for them.

Concerning the fact of not shaving off any hair, this is very important. Man's brain is like a huge transmitter, capable of sending out a multitude of very accurate waves and thoughts. In fact, telephathy is nothing more than that. But this type of transmitter requires antennas, and the hair and beard are these antennas. That is why one should not shave any hair off if one wants to make use of them. You have surely noticed that many of your scientists have long hair, and often a beard. The prophets and wise men also. Now you can better understand the reason why.

The child was born. It was Samson, whose story you know. He was able to communicate directly with 'God' by telepathy, thanks to his natural 'antennas', his hair. And the creators could then help him during difficult moments and produce marvels to reinforce his authority. But when Delilah cut his hair he could no longer ask for help. Then he had his eyes gouged by his enemies, but when his hair had grown again, he regained his 'strength'. That is to say, he could once again ask for help from the creators who then demolished the temple whose columns he was touching. All of this was attributed to Samson's 'strength'.

In Samuel 3, we find Elijah initiating Samuel to telepathy: the creators wanted to contact Samuel, and he thinks that Elijah is speaking to him. He 'hears voices'.

'Go, lie down: and it shall be if he call thee that thou shalt say, speak Yahwe for thy servant heareth'. Samuel 3:9.

This is something like amateur radio operators, one of whom might say: go ahead, I can hear you loud and clear. And the telepathic conversation begins.

'Samuel, Samuel...then Samuel answered, speak for thy servant heareth'.

In the episode where David challenges Goliath there is quite an interesting sentence: 'That he should defy the armies of the living God?' Samuel 17:26. Which shows the reality of the presence in that epoch of a 'God' quite palpable...

Telepathy as a means of communication between the creators and humans was only possible when the Elohim were in proximity to the earth. When they were on their distant planet, or elsewhere, they could not communicate in this way. This is why they installed a transmitter-receiver which was transported in the 'Ark of God', an apparatus containing its own atomic-powered cell. This is why in Samuel 1-5 and 6, when the Philistines stole the Ark of God, their idol Dagon lay face down on the ground before the Ark of Yahwe, following an electrical discharge caused by mishandling. They also received burns from the dangerous radiation of the radioactive products.

'And afflicted them with tumours.'

Even the Hebrews who had not taken precautions while handling the "Ark of God" were harmed.

'The oxen stumbled and Uzzah reached out to the

Ark of God and took hold of it. Yahwe was angry with Uzzah and struck him down there for his rash act. So he died there beside the Ark of God.' Samuel 6.

The Ark nearly fell over, and Uzzah, trying to hold it up, touched a dangerous part of the machine and was electrocuted.

In the book of Kings 1:2, we read in several places:

'And caught hold of the horns of the altar', which describes the manipulation of the transmitter-receiver levers in an effort to communicate with the creators.

The First Residence To Welcome The Elohim

The great king Solomon built a sumptuous residence to welcome the creators when they came to visit the earth.

'Yahwe said he resides in a cloud. I truly construct a house for you.'

'The glory of Yahwe has filled the house of Yahwe.' 'The cloud filled the house of Yahwe.' 1 Kings 6:13. 'I shall reside among the sons of Israel' 1 Kings 6.

So he lives in a cloud, or rather in a vessel that orbits the earth above the clouds. Imagine trying to make primitive people understand that.

'A man of god, sent by Yahwe, came from Judah to Bethel...he said,...the altar will be split apart. Jeroboam stretched out his hand from the altar and said "seize him!" But the hand he stretched out...shrivelled up so he could not pull it back and the altar split apart' 1 Kings 13.

With the help of an atomic disintegrator, one of the creators destroyed the altar, and burned the hand of one of the men who did not show respect for the creators. He returns to one of the Elohim's terrestrial camps by another route so that men would not discover them:

'Do not return again by the same way that thou camest. So he went by another way.'

An example of radio-control of animals by the use of electrodes as you are beginning to discover, is described in 1 Kings 17:

'And the ravens brought him bread and flesh in the morning, and bread and flesh in the evening.'

In view of the recent discoveries, as well as to give man an opportunity to evolve by himself, and to see if he would reach the age of scientific knowledge, the creators decided to appear less and less frequently. They also decided to use more discreet means of communication with humans, for example, the way they fed Elijah by the use of 'travelling ravens.'

This is the beginning of a gigantic experiment throughout the galaxy, where several humanities are competing. The creators decided to appear less often, all the while reinforcing the authority and the reputation of their ambassadors, the prophets, who performed 'miracles'. These miracles occurred simply because the prophets utilised scientific means incomprehensible to the people of that era.

'Look, your son is alive.'

'Now by this I know that thou art a man of God.'

Elijah had taken care of and healed a young dying child. Later he ordered two bull-calves to be placed on logs at Mount Carmel, one to be consecrated to the idol Baal, and the other to the creators. The one that would light up by itself would be the one true 'God'.

Naturally, at a moment agreed upon in advance between Elijah and the creators, the log destined to them kindled even though the wood was wet. This was accomplished by a powerful beam similar to a laser beam, which was emitted from a vessel hidden in the clouds.

'Then the fire of Yahwe fell and consumed the whole offering, and the wood, and the stones, and the dust, and licked up the water that was in the trench.'

Elijah The Messenger

The creators paid particular attention to Elijah.

'An angel touched him and said, "Arise and eat." At his bedside was a pancake and a jar of water. All this happened in the desert....'

'And behold Yahwe passed by, and a great and strong wind rent the mountains, and broke the rocks in front of Yahwe. But Yahwe is not in the wind. And after the wind came an earthquake but Yahwe was not in the earthquake; and after the earthquake came a fire; but Yahwe was not in the fire; and after the fire, a still small voice.' 1 Kings 19.

There you have the exact description of the landing of a machine similar to one of your rockets. Then further on the appearance of the creators is described:

'I saw Yahwe sitting on his throne, and all the army of heaven standing by him.' 1 Kings 22.

The creators once again used telepathy, group telepathy this time, so that none of the prophets could predict the truth to the King.

'I will be a lying spirit in the mouths of all his prophets.'

In the second chapter of Kings, there is further proof of the protection the creators gave to Elijah.

'If I am a man of God, may fire fall from heaven and consume you and your company! Fire fell from heaven and consumed the officer and his fifty men.' This operation happened again, but the third time, 'The angel of Yahwe said unto Elijah: go down with him and be not afraid of him.'

In the second book of Kings, Chapter 2, Elijah is invited aboard a spacecraft which takes off, bringing him along.

'When Yahwe would take up Elijah into heaven by a whirlwind.'

'There appeared a chariot of fire, and horses of fire, and parted them both asunder (Elijah and Elisha) and Elijah went up by a whirlwind into heaven.'

This is a clear description of a spacecraft taking off, and when the narrator speaks of horses of fire, he is referring to the fire and smoke which was emitted from the blast-pipes. If you showed certain South American or African tribesmen a rocket taking off, they would be incapable of understanding this scientific phenomena in a rational way, and would look upon it as something supernatural, mystical, and divine. When they return to their tribes, they would speak of fire-horses and chariots.

Further on in the book of Kings 2, verse 4, Elisha, like his father, proceeds to perform a 'resurrection', and he heals and brings back to life a child who was dead. This happens quite frequently at the present time by the use of mouth to mouth resuscitation and heart massage, often bringing back to life a person whose cardiac muscle has ceased to function.

Then Elisha multiplies the bread.

The Multiplication of Bread

'The man of God brought twenty barley loaves, but his servant said: How can I feed one hundred people with twenty loaves? They will eat and there will be some left over. So he set it before them and they ate and left some over, as Yahwe had said.'

The creators had brought synthetic dehydrated food with them, which, when added to water, increased to five times its original volume. So with twenty small "loaves" of bread there was enough food for a hundred people. You already know about the little vitamin pills which your first astronauts were nourished with. They take very little space but contain all the necessary nutritional elements. One pill is enough to feed one man. A quantity equivalent in volume to one small loaf of bread is enough to feed five men. Therefore, twenty loaves are sufficient to feed one hundred men.

But the people of Israel, who adored metal idols, were cannibals and had become completely immoral, much to the disgust of the creators.

'So was Israel carried away out of their land.' 2 Kings 17:23.

In the book of Isaiah you again find:

'In the year of King Oziah's death I saw Adonai seated on a throne, high and exalted...above him stood the seraphim: each one has six wings, one pair covered his face, and one pair his feet, and one pair was spread in flight.' Isaiah 6.

This described the creators dressed in one-piece suits with six small jet-engines, two in the back, two on the arms, and two on the feet, which were for directional purposes.

That was the beginning of the dispersion of the Israelites , whose civilisation, instead of progressing, was in constant recession, contrary to their neighbours who took advantage of it.

'Listen, a noise on the mountains like that of a great multitude! An uproar among kingdoms like nations massing together! Yahwe is mustering an army for war. They come from far away lands from the ends of the heavens, Yahwe and the weapons of his wrath to destroy the whole country.' Isaiah 13.

The whole truth is written here, but it was necessary to read between the lines and ... understand. 'They come from a far country, from the end of heaven.' which is clear enough.

'You thought in your own mind, I will ascend to

heaven, I will raise my throne above the stars of God.'

This alludes to the scientists who had disappeared, having accumulated sufficient scientific knowledge to undertake a trip to the creator's planet, and who were destroyed in Sodom and Gomorrah. The army of the heavens at that time is described here, when they arrived with their weapons of wrath to destroy the whole country. Those men of Sodom and Gomorrah who said:

'I will rise above the cloud-banks and make myself like the most high' Isaiah 14.

But the destruction prevented the humans from equalling their creators 'The most high'.

'He made the world a wilderness....' Isaiah 14.

The nuclear explosion is described further on:

'For the cry is gone round about the border of Moab; the howling thereof unto Eglaim and unto the well of Beerelim the cry thereof...for the waters of Dimon are filled with blood... Isaiah 15:8-9.

'A few were saved because they sheltered in blockhouses.'

'Go my people, enter your rooms and shut your doors behind you; withdraw a brief while until the wrath has gone by.' Isaiah 26.

The Flying Saucers of Ezekiel

It is in the book of Ezekiel that we find the most interesting description of one of our flying machines:

'I looked, and I saw a windstorm coming out of the north, an immense cloud with flashing lightning and surrounded by brilliant light. The centre of the fire looked like glowing metal and in the fire was what looked like four living creatures. In appearance their form was that of a man, but each of them had four faces and four wings. Their legs were straight, their feet were like those of a calf and gleamed like burnished bronze. Under their wings on their four sides they had the hands of a man. All four of them had faces and wings, and their wings touched one another. Each one went straight ahead; they did not turn as they moved.

Their faces looked like this: Each of the four had the face of a man, and on the right side each had the face of a lion, and on the left the face of an ox; each also had the face of an eagle. Such were their faces. Their wings were spread out upwards; each had two wings one touching the wing of another creature on either side, and two wings covering its body. Each one went straight ahead. Wherever the spirit would go they would go, without turning as they went.

The appearance of the living creatures was like burning coals of fire or like torches. Fire moved back and forth among the creatures; it was bright, and lightning flashed out of it. The creatures sped back and forth like flashes of lightning.

As I looked at the living creatures, I saw a wheel on the ground beside each creature with its four faces. This was the appearance and structure of the wheels. They sparkled like chrysolite, and all four looked alike. Each appeared to be made like a wheel intersecting a wheel. As they moved, they would go in any one of four directions the creatures faced; the wheels did not turn about as the creatures went. Their rims were high and awesome and all four rims were full of eyes all around.

When the living creatures moved, the wheels beside them moved; and when the living creatures rose from the ground, the wheels also rose. Wherever the spirit would go, they would go, and the wheels would rise along with them, because the spirit of the living creatures was in the wheels. When the creatures moved they also moved; when the creatures stood still, they also stood still; and when the creatures rose from the ground, the wheels rose along with them, because the spirit of the living creatures was in the wheels.

Spread out above the heads of the living creatures was what looked like an expanse, sparkling like ice and awesome. Under the expanse their wings were stretched out one towards the other, and each had two wings covering its body. When the creatures moved, I heard the sound of their wings, like the roar of rushing waters, like the voice of the Almighty, like the tumult of an army. When they stood still, they lowered their wings.

Then there came a voice from above the expanse over their heads as they stood with lowered wings. Above the expanse over their heads was what looked like a throne of sapphire, and high above on the throne was a figure like that of a man.' Ezekiel 1.

There you have a description which could not be more precise of the landing of the creators in their flying machine. The 'windstorm' is the trace of smoke (vapor trail) that our present day planes leave behind them at high altitudes. Then the machine appeared with its blinking light, the 'flashing lightning'

and 'glowing metal'.

Later, four creators appear with antigravity suits and small directional jet-engines, described as the 'wings' on their metal suits, 'their feet...gleamed like burnished bronze'. You have surely noticed how shiny your astronauts' suits are. As for the 'flying saucer', the 'wheel', their appearance and their operation were not so badly described, when you consider it is a primitive man who is speaking.... 'As it were a wheel in the middle of a wheel...they turned not when they went.' In the center of the 'flying saucer' very similar to the one in which we are now, is the habitable section, the 'rims'. 'All four rims were full of eyes, all around'. In the same way that our clothing has evolved, and we no longer wear those cumbersome suits, our vessels had portholes, the 'eyes' around the 'rims', for we had not yet discovered how to see through metallic walls by modifying their atomic structures at will.

The 'flying saucers' stay near the creators to help them in case of need, for they are supplying them with various materials, and are checking the large intergalactic vessel above them. Other creators inside the vessels are directing them. 'The spirit of the living creature was in the wheels.' Evidently the suit is also described with its four portholes similar to those of our first diving-suits. 'Each of them had four faces ... and they did not turn as they moved.'

The small 'saucers' are something like 'lems', small vehicles with short ranges used for exploration missions. Above them the larger interplanetary vessel waits. 'Spread out above the heads of the living creatures was what looked like an expanse, sparkling like ice and awesome.... Above the expanse over their heads was what looked like a throne of sapphire, and high above on the throne was a figure like that of a man.' The latter on the large vessel was supervising and coordinating the work of the creators.

Ezekiel, frightened, fell flat on his face, because all those mysterious events had to come from no one but 'God ' but one of the creators said to him, 'Man,' he said, 'stand up and let me talk with you...listen to what I say and eat what I give you.' Ezekiel 2.

This is an image, like the 'eating' from the scientific tree of good and evil. It is in fact an intellectual 'food'. It was indeed a book that was given: 'then I saw a hand stretched out to me holding a scroll...it was written all over on both sides.'

There was writing on both sides, a very surprising thing at that time when usually on one side of a parchment was written on. Then the scroll is 'eaten'. This means that Ezekiel acquired its meaning, and what he learned is what you are learning now about man's origin. It was so exciting and so encouraging that he said, 'So I ate it, and it tasted as sweet as honey'

Then Ezekiel is transported in the creators' vessel to the place where he was to spread the good news.

'Then the spirit took me up...and took me away.... I heard behind me a voice of a great rushing.' Ezekiel 3.

Further on, the 'prophet' is transported once again by the creators' flying machine.

'And the spirit lifted me up between the earth and the heaven, and brought me in the vision of God to Jerusalem.' Ezekiel 8.

Ezekiel noticed afterwards that under their 'wings' the 'Cherubim' had hands like those of men.

'And there appeared in the Cherubim the form of a man's hand under their wings.'

'While I watched, the Cherubim spread their wings and rose from the ground and as they went, the wheels went with them.' Ezekiel 10.

'The spirit lifted me up, and brought me.' Ezekiel 11.

'The glory of Yahwe went up from the midst of the city, and stopped above the mountain which was on the east side of the city. Afterwards the spirit took me up and brought me into Chaldea.' Ezekiel 11.

There you have the many journeys of Ezekiel in the creators' flying machines.

'Yahwe set me down in the middle of the valley.' Ezekiel 37.

And then a 'miracle' will happen. The creators will restore to life humans whose only remains are their bones. As mentioned earlier, in each cell of a living being there is contained all the information necessary to reconstruct it completely. You have only to place a single cell, such as from the bone remains, in a machine that provides all the living matter required to reconstruct that original being. The machine supplies the substance, and the cell supplies all of the necessary information for the plans by which the being would be constructed, just as a spermatozoon contains all the information necessary to create a living being, even to the colour of the hair and the eyes.

'Son of man, can these bones live? There was a noise, and behold a shaking...the sinews and the flesh came up upon them, and the skin covered them ...they came to life and stood up upon their feet, an exceeding great army' Ezekiel 37.

All this is very easy to do, and you will do it some day. This is the origin of the very ancient ritual of making the burials of great men as protected as possible, so that one day they may be brought back to life, and perpetually so. This is a part of the secret of the 'tree of life', the secret of eternity.

Ezekiel is again carried away in a spacecraft, which takes him near a man wearing a space-suit.

'...and brought me...and set me upon a very high mountain, on whose south side were some buildings that looked like a city...and behold, there was a man whose appearance was like the appearance of brass ....' Ezekiel 40.

This 'city' is one of the earth bases that the creators used at that time,. which were always situated on very high mountains in order not to be disturbed by men. The man 'whose appearance was like the appearance of brass', is of course wearing a metallic suit...in the same way as we were mistaken for children or cherubs due to our small structure.

The priests in charge of serving the creators in their

terrestrial residence, the 'temple' visited by Ezekiel, were wearing aseptic clothing when performing their duties, and those clothes had to stay always in the temple, so as to avoid being contaminated by germs dangerous to the creators.

'When the priests have entered the holy place, they shall not enter the outer court without leaving here the garments they have worn while performing their duties, for these are holy.'

They should have written 'for these garments are pure or sterile' but that was incomprehensible for primitives who deified all that was told or shown to them at that period.

In Ezekiel 43, the big vessel, respectfully called 'the glory of God' approached.

'And I saw the glory of the God of Israel coming from the east; and his voice was like the noise of many waters; and the earth shined with his glory.'

They did not want to be disturbed.

'This gate is to remain shut, it shall not be opened, and no man shall enter in by it; because Yahwe, God of Israel, has entered in by it, therefore it shall be shut.'

Only the 'prince' is allowed to come and speak with the creators.

'The prince himself is the only one who may sit inside the gateway to eat in the presence of Yahwe'.

But the Prince had to pass through a chamber, where he was aseptisized by special rays.

'He shall enter by way of the porch of that gate, and shall go out the same way.'

The Levite 'priests' were there to serve the creators.

'They shall come near to me to minister unto me, and they shall come before me to offer unto me the fat and the blood . . . and they alone shall come near to my table, to minister unto me . . . .'

'That when they enter the gates of the inner court, they must be clothed with linen garments . . . they shall not gird themselves with anything that causeth sweat.'

The odour of earth man's perspiration was very unpleasant to the creators.

'The best of all your first fruits . . . and the first of your dough you will give to the priests so a blessing may rest on your household.'

The supplying of fresh products for the creators continued in this way.

In the third chapter of Daniel, King Nebuchadnezzar condemned three men to the stake for not adoring a metal God instead of the creators, whose existence they were aware of. But the three men were saved by one of the creators who came to their aid in the glowing fire and with a method of repulsion and freezing, repelled the heat and the flames from around them, allowing them to walk away without having suffered any burns at all.

'. . . I see four men loose, walking in the midst of the fire, and they have no hurt; and the form of the fourth looks like the son of Gods . . . .' Daniel 3.

Further on, Daniel is cast into the lion's den, but the lions do not harm him. There again, nothing complicated, a paralyzing beam allowed them to get Daniel out of the den unharmed.

'My God has sent his angel to shut the lion's mouth.' Daniel 6.

In the tenth chapter of Daniel you will find another interesting description of a creator: 'I looked up and saw a man . . . his body gleamed like topaz, his face shone like lightning, his eyes flamed like torches, his arms and feet sparkled like a disc of bronze; and when he spoke his voice sounded like the voice of a multitude.'

The Last Judgement

If the Hebrews were dominated by the Persians and the Greeks it was because of their lack of faith. Consequently, the Elohim sent some of their 'angels' amongst the two peoples to help them progress technically. This explains the great moments in the history of those two civilisations. The angel Michael was the leader of the delegation for helping the Persians.

'Michael, one of the chief princes, came to help the kingdom of Persia.' Daniel 10.

In chapter 12 of Daniel, the resurrection is again mentioned.

'And many of them that sleep in the dust of the earth shall awake, some to everlasting life, and some to shame and everlasting contempt.' Daniel 12.

The 'Last judgement' will enable great men to live again. Those people who have been positive towards humanity, and who have truly believed in their creators and followed their commandments, will be welcomed with great joy by the people of the era when this will happen. On the other hand, all the wicked people will be ashamed before their judges, and will live in eternal regret as an example for the rest of humanity.

'The wise leaders shall shine like the bright vault of heaven and those who have guided the people on the true path shall be like the stars for ever and ever.' Daniel 12.

The geniuses will be the most highly esteemed, and the most highly rewarded. The just men, having allowed the geniuses to blossom, or the truth to triumph, will also be rewarded.

'But you, Daniel, keep the words secret and seal the book till the time of the end; many will seek here and there and knowledge shall be increased.' Daniel 12.

These words will only be understood when man will have reached a sufficient scientific level, and that time has arrived and all this will happen.

'When the power of the holy people ceases to be dispersed.'

This will be when the people of Israel will recover their land after the long dispersion. The State of Israel was created some thirty years ago, at the same time as the explosion of man's scientific knowledge.

'Go your way, Daniel, for the words are kept secret and sealed till the time of the end.' Daniel 12.

All this, could not be understood at that time.

Now all can be understood. In recent years scientific progress and the beginning of space exploration by humans have been such, that everything seems possible for man. Nothing surprises people anymore, for they are used to seeing many wonders happening before their very eyes on television. They can learn without astonishment that they are really made in the image of 'God', their Almighty Creator, even as far as their scientific possibilities are concerned. The 'miracles' become understandable.

In Jonah, the 'big fish' that swallows the prophet is very interesting indeed. Jonah was thrown into the water from a small boat.

'Now Yahwe had prepared a great fish to swallow up Jonah, and Jonah was in the belly of the fish for three days and three nights.'

The 'great fish' was in fact a submarine as you know them now. But for the men of that time it could only be a 'great fish', even though the gastric juices of such a fish would have digested the man quickly, without any hope of returning to open air. What is more, it would have to have air in order for Jonah to breathe .... In that submarine the creators were able to carry on a conversation with Jonah and learn about current political evolution.

'And Yahwe spoke unto the fish, and it vomited out Jonah upon the dry land.'

The submarine came close to the shore and Jonah was back on land.

In Zachariah 5, there is another description of a flying machine.

'I looked up again and saw a flying scroll, twenty cubits long (9 metres) and ten cubits wide (4.5 metres).' Zachariah 5.

A little further on the women of the creators appear for the first time.

'. . . beyond, there came out two women, and the wind was in their wings; for they had wings like the wings of a stork . . . ' Zachariah 5.

Two female companions were with the creators, both equipped with autonomous flying suits, appear before Zachariah.

In Psalms 8, it is said about man, 'Thou hast made him a little less than the Elohim.'

Men are nearly as strong intellectually as their creators. Those who recopied the texts did not dare to write 'equal to the Elohim' as it had been dictated.

'His starting point is from the end of the heaven, and his circuit unto the ends of it.' Psalms 19.

The creators came from a planet very far away from the earth's orbit.

'In the heavens he has pitched a tent for the sun.' Psalms 19.

Another allusion to the pile of earth which was created when the oceans covered the earth and formed the original continent.

'Yahwe looks out from heaven; and watches all mankind; he surveys from his dwelling place all the inhabitants of earth.' Psalms 33.

The creators watch humanity's behaviour as they have always done, from their flying vessels.

Satan

In the book of Job, Chapter 1, you have the explanation of Satan.

'Now there was a day when the sons of Elohim came to present themselves before Yahwe, and Satan also came with them.' Job 1.

Elohim means literally 'those who came from the sky' in Hebrew. The sons of Elohim, in other words, the creators who watch humans, report regularly to their planet of origin that most of them venerate and love the Elohim. But one of them called Satan, was part of a group that had always condemned the creation of other intelligent beings on a planet as close to theirs as earth is, seeing a possible threat in it. That is why, seeing Job's devotion, one of the best examples of men loving their creators, he said:

'Satan answered to Yahwe and said: has not Job good reason to fear Elohim? .... But stretch out your hand and touch all that he has, and then he will curse you to your face. And Yahwe said to Satan: so be it. All that he has is in your hands; only Job himself you must not touch.' Job 1.

Hearing Satan's assertion that had Job not been rich, he would not have loved his creators, the government gave full power to Satan in order that he may ruin Job. It shall then be seen if he still venerates his creators, and that is why he must not be killed.

Seeing Job's stubbornness in respecting his creators, even when he was ruined, the government triumphs over the opposition, Satan. But the latter replied that Job had lost many things but was still in good health. The government gives Satan 'carte blanche' as long as he does not kill him.

'He is in your hands; but, save his life.'

Again, in the book of Job, a small sentence in Chapter 37 is very interesting.

'Can you beat out the vault of the skies, as he does, hard as a mirror of cast metal?'

Is man capable of making 'solid clouds', in reality flying metallic vessels. Men of that time think it is possible for no one but God. Nevertheless, it exists . . . . at present.

Finally, in view of Job's humility, the creators heal him, give back to him his wealth, his children and his health.

Men Could Not Understand

In the book of Tobias, a robot named Raphael also comes to test the human's reaction towards their creators. Once he had accomplished his mission, he leaves, after having proven who he is.

'Everyday, I appeared unto you but neither did I eat nor drink . . . . I am ascending to him who sent me. Write down these things that have happened to you.' Tobias 12.

All of this is easy to see in the writings. But then again one must try to understand.

'I shall tell you what wisdom is, and what is her

origin, and I will not hide from you the mysteries of Elohim, but will reveal from the beginning of her birth, and bring the knowledge of her to light, and will not pass over the truth.' Wisdom of Solomon 6.

When the time comes, 'wisdom', the science which allowed all this to exist, will be known by man. The biblical writings will be the proof of all this.

'For by the greatness of the beauty, and of the creature, the creators of them may be seen, so as to be known thereby.' Wisdom of Solomon 13.

It was rather simple to see the truth, to recognise the creators by observing the created thing.

'And who by these good things that are seen could not understand him that is.' Wisdom of Solomon 13.

In order not to be disturbed by humans, the creators built their bases on high mountains, where we now find traces of great civilisations, (Himalayas, Peru, etc.), as well as on the bottom of the sea. Progressively the mountain stations were abandoned for submarine bases less accessible to men. The creators who had been banished in the beginning hid themselves in the oceans.

'In that day Yahwe with his sore and great and strong sword shall punish Leviathan the piercing serpent, even Leviathan that crooked serpent; and he shall slay the dragon that is in the sea.' Isaiah 27.

At that time the government of their planet wanted to destroy the creators of man. It was not easy to see clearly among all those wonders, so of course the creators were deified and considered as something abstract for men were unable to understand scientific facts.

'And the book is delivered to him that is not learned, saying: Read this, I pray thee: and he said I am not learned.' Isaiah 29.

For a long time, men have had the truth in their hands but could not understand it before they were able to 'read it' i.e. to be sufficiently evolved scientifically.

'Every man is brutish in his lack of knowledge ....' Jeremiah 10.

Science enabled the creators to create and will enable men to do the same.

'Yahwe possessed me in the beginning of his way, before his work of old. I was set up from everlasting, from the beginning, or ever the earth was .... When he prepared the heavens I was there .... When he gave to the sea his decree that the waters should not pass his commandment, then I was with him, as one brought up with him. And I was daily his delights rejoicing always before him; rejoicing in the habitable part of his earth, and my delights were with the sons of men.' Proverbs 8-2.

Intelligence and science, these are two virtues that enabled the creators to create 'the land mass', the unique continent and the living beings they set on it. And now this intelligence and this spirit leads the human brain to a repetition of their creator's acts. Since the beginning of time it has been so, men create other men, similar to those on other planets. The cycle continues. Some die, others take over. We are your creators and you will create other men.

'That which has been is now; and that which is to be has already been . . . .' Ecclesiastes 3:15.

'so that a man has no preeminence above a beast: for all is vanity' Ecclesiastes 3:19.

The animals were also created, and will be re-created, just as with man, neither more, nor less. The species that disappear will live again when you know how to recreate them.

We the creators will only show ourselves officially if mankind is grateful to us for having created them. We are afraid that humans will hold a grudge against us. We would like to open contact with you and benefit you with our considerable advance in scientific knowledge, if we were sure that you would not turn against us, and that you would love us as your fathers.

'Woe to him who quarrels with his maker. Will the clay ask the potter what he is making or his handiwork say to him you have no skill? Woe unto him that sais to his father, what are you begetting?' Isaiah 45.

'I have tested you in the furnace of affliction, for my own sake, for my own sake I did it.' Isaiah 48.

It is with the fear of not being loved by humans that the creators have let them progress scientifically by themselves, almost without helping them.

The emblem you see engraved on this machine, and on my suit, represents the truth; it is also the emblem of the Jewish people; the Star of David, which means: that which is above is like that which is below, and in the centre of which is the 'Swastika' which means that everything is cyclic, the top becoming the bottom, and the bottom becoming the top. The origins and the destiny of the creators and humans are similar and united.

'Do you not know? Have you not heard? Were you not told from the beginning? Have you not understood from the foundation of the earth?' Isaiah 40:21.

The trace of the creators' bases on high mountains is mentioned in the book of Amos.

'He who marches over the heights of the earth.' Amos 4:13.

The creators had seven bases in all: '. . . those seven; they are the eyes of Yahwe which run to and fro through the whole world.' Zachariah 4:10.

That is the origin of the seven-branched candlestick, the meaning of which had been lost. In the beginning there was, at the creators' headquarters, a switchboard with seven lighted switches enabling them to stay in contact with the other bases, and with the interplanetary vessel orbiting on earth.

Concerning the allusion to telepathy:

'Before a word is on my tongue you know it completely O Yahwe you hem me in - behind and before; you have laid your hand on me. Such knowledge is too wonderful for me; it is high, I cannot attain it.' Psalms 139: 4-6.

At that time telepathy was unimaginable, 'such knowledge is too wonderful for me'.

Astronomy and interplanetary journeys were also unthinkable at that time.

'He numbers the stars one by one and calls them each by name. Great is our Lord, and great his power, his understanding is infinite.' Psalms 147: 4-5.

They were also unable to understand telecommunication.

'He sends his command to the ends of the earth, and his word runs swiftly.' Psalms 147.

We are getting to a decisive stage in the creators' work, its orientation. They then decided to let men progress scientifically without ever intervening directly. They understood that they themselves had been created in the same way, and that by creating similar beings, they were allowing the cycle to continue.

But first, in order for the truth to be spread throughout the world, they decided to send a 'Messiah' who would be able to spread around the world what the people of Israel are the only ones to know, in preparation for the day of the revelation of the original mystery, when things can be seen in light of scientific progress. Then, they announced him.

'But out of you, Bethlehem, shall come forth a governor for Israel, and whose roots are far back in the past, in days gone by. He shall stand, and be their shepherd in the strength of Yahwe . . . to the ends of the earth, and he shall be a man of peace.' Micah 5:2.

'Exult, daughters of Jerusalem, here is your King coming forth to you . . . humble and carried on a mule . . . he will dictate peace to the nations, his empire will cover from sea to sea.'

CHAPTER IV
THE USEFULNESS OF CHRIST

The Conception

The Initiation

Parallel Humanities

Scientific Miracles

Deserving the Inheritance

The Conception

Christ was to spread the truth about the writings of the Bible throughout the world, so that it could serve as proof to all of humanity when the scientific age would explain everything to man.

The creators therefore decided to bring to the earth a child who would be born of an earth-woman, and one of their own. The child in question would inherit certain telepathic faculties which men lack.

'She was found with child by the Holy Ghost.' Matthew 1.

Obviously the fiancé of Mary who was the chosen earth-woman, found these tidings a bit hard to take, but: 'Behold, the angel of the Lord appeared unto him.' Matthew 1:20.

One of the creators appeared to him to explain that Mary would bring forth the son of "God".

The prophets, who were in contact with the creators, came from very far away to see the divine child. One of the spacecrafts guided them: 'We observed the rising of his star, and we have come to pay him homage.'

'And the star which they had seen at its rising went ahead of them until it stopped above the place where the child lay.' Matthew 2.

And the creators watched over the child:

'And the angel of the Lord appeared in a dream to Joseph, saying arise and take the child and his mother, and flee into Egypt, and remain there until I tell you; for Herod will seek the child to destroy him.' Matthew 2:13.

The King was not too happy about the child-king who had just been born on his territory, and whom the prophets had announced. When King Herod died, the creators told Joseph that he could return to Israel:

'But when Herod was dead, an angel of the Lord appeared in a dream to Joseph in Egypt . . . saying: Arise, and take the child and his mother, and go into the land of Israel, for those who sought the child's life are dead.'

The Initiation

When he became of age, Jesus was led to the creators so they could reveal his true identity to him, introduce him to his father, reveal his mission, and teach him various scientific techniques.

'Heaven opened; and he saw the spirit of God descending like a dove to alight upon him; and a voice from heaven was heard, saying: This is my son, my beloved, on whom my favour rests. Jesus was then led away by the spirit into the wilderness to be tempted by the devil.'

The devil, 'Satan' the creator of whom we spoke previously, is still convinced that nothing good can come of man. He is 'Satan' the skeptic. He was supported by the government's opposition on our distant planet. Satan tests Jesus to find out if his intelligence is positive, and if he really loves and respects his creators. Having found out that one could have complete confidence in Jesus, he was allowed to go and accomplish his mission.

In order to rally most of the people to him, he performed 'miracles', which in reality were applications of the scientific teachings shown to him by the creators.

'Sufferers from every kind of illness were all brought to him, and he cured them.' Matthew 4.

'Blessed are the poor in spirit.' Matthew 5:3.

This sentence has been incorrectly interpreted as: Blessed are the poor in spirit. The original meaning was that if the poor have spirit, then they will be happy. It has nothing to do with the last sentence.

Then he tells his apostles that they must spread the truth throughout the world:

In a prayer called 'our Father' the truth is stated literally:

'Thy kingdom come . . . thy will be done on earth as it is in heaven.' Matthew 6:10.

In heaven, on the creators' planet, the scientists ended up by ruling and then created other intelligent beings. The same thing will happen on earth. The torch will be taken up again. This prayer, which has been repeated again and again without understanding its profound meaning, now takes its full meaning 'On earth, as it is in heaven.'

Amongst other things, Jesus had been taught how to speak convincingly through telepathic group hypnosis:

'And it came to pass when Jesus had finished these words, that the crowds were astonished at his teachings . . . for he was teaching them as one having authority, and not as their scribes . . . .' Matthew 7.

He continued healing the sick with the aid of the creators, who directed some concentrated beams from a distance:

'A leper approached him . . . Jesus stretched out his hand, touched him, and said; Indeed I will, be clean again. And his leprosy was cured immediately.'

And he did the same for a man who was completely paralysed. The operation was carried out from a distance by a concentrated ray, something like the laser, burning only one spot through the layers.

'Arise and walk . . . and he rose.'

Further on in the book of Matthew, Jesus announces his mission: 'I did not come to invite virtuous people, but the sinners.'

He did not come for the people of Israel, who knew of the existence of the creators, but rather so that this knowledge would be spread throughout the world.

Later, there were more 'miracles' somewhat similar to the first ones, all of which were medically performed.

Nowadays, there are heart transplants and transplants of other organs; leprosy and other similar illnesses are cured, and people are brought out of a coma with appropriate care. These would be considered as miracles by primitive people.

At that time, humans were primitive, and the creators were similar to men of your present 'civilised' nations, although more advanced scientifically.

Further on we find an allusion to the creators among whom is the real father of Jesus:

'Whoever then will acknowledge me before men, I will acknowledge him before my father in heaven.' Matthew 10:32.

'Before my father who is in heaven.'

This says it all. In fact, 'God' is not impalpable or immaterial. He is in heaven. This is obviously incomprehensible to those people who believed that the stars are attached to a heavenly canopy just like numerous light bulbs revolving around the center of the world: the earth. Now on the other hand, since the beginning of space travel, and a more profound understanding of its immensity, the texts are brought to light in a completely different way.

Parallel Humanities

Chapter 13 is an important chapter, where Jesus explains in a parable:

'The sower went out to sow.' Matthew 13:3. It explains how the creators left their planet to create life on another world.

'And as he sowed, some seeds fell by the wayside, and the birds came and ate them up.' Matthew 13:4.

'And other seeds fell upon rocky ground, where they had not much earth . . . but when the sun rose they were scorched.' Matthew 13: 5-6.

'Other seeds fell among thorns which grew up and

choked the plants' Matthew 13:7.

'And other seeds fell upon good ground, and yielded fruit, some a hundredfold, some sixtyfold, and some thirtyfold . . . . He who has ears to hear, let him hear.' Matthew 13: 8-9.

This is an allusion to the various attempts to create life on other planets:

Three of them failed. The first failed because some 'birds' came and ate the seeds, which was in fact a failure due to the proximity of this planet to the creators' planet. Those who were against the creation of men similar to them saw a possible threat in the experiment and therefore they came to destroy the creation. The second attempt was made on a planet too near a sun which was too hot; therefore, their creation was destroyed by noxious radiations. On the other hand, the third attempt was made 'among the thorns' on the planet which was far too humid, where the plant life was so powerful that it destroyed the equilibrium and the animal world.

This world of plants still exists. But finally, the fourth attempt was successful on the 'good ground'.

And an important fact is that there were three successes, which means that on two other planets relatively near, there are similar beings who were created by the same creators.

'Hear they who have ears': understand those who can . . . . When the time comes, those who try to understand, will . . . . the others, those who look without really seeing and hear without really listening and understanding, those will never understand the truth.

Those who will have proven their intelligence by themselves will be worthy of the creators' help and therefore will be helped:

'For the man who has will be given more, till he has enough and to spare; and the man who has not will forfeit even what he has.'

The people who will not be able to prove their intelligence will be destroyed. Humans have nearly proven that they are worthy of being recognised by their creators as their equals. They lack only . . . a little love. Love for each other, and particularly for their creators.

'It is given unto you to know the mysteries of the Kingdom of Heaven.'

The three planets on which life has been created were to compete with each other. The one in which humanity would make the most scientific progress, thereby proving their intelligence, would benefit from the creators' inheritance on the day of the 'last judgement'. On the condition that they are not aggressive towards them. This will be a day when their knowledge will have reached a sufficiently high level. Humans on earth are not very far away from that day.

The human genius is: 'the smallest of all the seeds, but when it grows up it is larger than any herb and becomes a tree, so that the birds of the air come and dwell in its branches.' Matthew 13:32.

About the 'birds of the sky': the creators will come and 'lodge' in its branches, and give their knowledge to the humans when they will be worthy of it.

'The Kingdom of Heaven is like leaven which a woman took and buried in three measures of flour, until all of it was leavened.' Matthew 13:33.

Another allusion to the three worlds in which the creators are waiting for science to bloom:

'I will utter things hidden since the foundation of the world.' Matthew 13:35.

One of the most important things is that planets have a life span, and one day they will become unsuitable to support life. At that time, humans must have reached a sufficient level of scientific knowledge to undertake a move to another planet, or to create a humanoid form of life adapted to another world, in order to assure its survival, if it cannot adapt itself elsewhere. If the environment cannot be adapted to man, man must become adapted to a new environment.

For example, before man's extinction, he would have to create another race of man able to live in a totally different atmosphere, and who would inherit the knowledge of the creators, in this case man, before his expiration.

So that the inheritance is not completely lost, the creators put life on three worlds, so that the best one only will be entitled to the inheritance:

'So will it be at the end of the world: the angels will go out and separate the wicked from among the just.' Matthew 13:49.

The passage concerning the multiplication of bread has previously been explained. It consists of concentrated food products with the appearance of large pills similar to the ones the astronauts use which contain all the vital elements. The 'Holy Bread' and their form remind us of these pills. With the equivalent of a few loaves of bread, there is enough to feed thousands of men.

Scientific Miracles

When Jesus walked on the water the creators supported him by using an anti-gravitation beam which cancels the effects of weight on a precise point.

'He came to them, walking upon the sea.'

This created a turbulence described as follows:

'But seeing the wind was strong, Peter was afraid . . . and when they got into the boat, the wind fell.' Matthew 14:32.

The 'wind ceased' when they got into the boat because the beam was switched off when Jesus reached the boat. Another scientific 'Miracle'. There are no miracles, but only differences in levels of civilisations. If you landed at the time of Jesus with a cosmic vessel, or even a simple helicopter, you would, in the eyes of the people of that time, be performing miracles, in spite of your limited scientific level. By producing artificial light, by coming from the sky, by driving a car, by watching television, or even by killing a bird with a gun, you would have provided people of that period with unexplainable phenomena and therefore they would have dismissed these technical advances as a 'divine' or supernatural force. It would be fair to say that there is probably the same gap between you and the men in the time of Jesus, as between you and us. We can still do things which you would consider 'miracles'. But the most developed ones among you would not consider them 'miracles'. Over the last few decades or more, man has grapsed the tremendous magnitude of life and development possible through scientific investigation and exploration and is actively pursuing scientific laws and possibilities instead of dumbly prostrating himself on his belly and bringing offerings. Our knowledge, however, remains such that if we decided to perform a few 'miracles', not even your most eminent scientists would be able to understand how we performed them. A few particularly well-developed minds would be able to cope with them, but crowds would simply panic. We are still able to astonish these crowds who are no longer easily shocked.

It is necessary for people to know now that there is not an immaterial 'God' but that there are men who have created other men in their image. In Chapter 17 of Matthew, the creators appear once again:

'. . . Jesus took Peter, James and his brother John, and led them up a high mountain by themselves . . . and was transfigured before them. And his face shone as the Sun, and his raiment was white as the light . . . and behold there appeared to them Moses and Elijah talking together with him . . . behold a bright cloud over-shadowed them, and behold, a voice out of the cloud said: This is my beloved son . . . hear him.' Matthew 17:1-5.

This scene happens at night, and the apostles are all frightened to see Jesus illuminated by the powerful projectors of the spacecraft, out of which Moses and Elijah stepped, still alive, thanks to the tree of life from which they benefited. Immortality is a scientific reality, even if it does not correspond to man's idea of immortality.

The sentence:

'But many who are first now will be last, and many who are last now will be first . . ' meaning that the created shall become creators just as the creators were created. Matthew 19:30.

Deserving the Inheritance

According to the Gospel of Matthew, Chapter 25, it is said that the three planets must make scientific progress, and that they would be judged one day. We read in the parable:

'For it is like a man going abroad, who called his servants and handed over his goods to them.' Matthew 25:14.

'and to one he gave five talents;

'to another, two;

'to another one.'

'And then he went on his journey . . . and he who had received the five talents went and traded with them, and gained five more.'

'In like manner, he who had received the two gained two more.'

'But he who had received the one returned only one talent.'

'Take away therefore the talent from him, and give it to him who has the ten talents .... For to everyone who has shall be given, and he shall have abundance, but from him who does not have, even that which he seems to have shall be taken away.'

Out of the three worlds where life has been created, the one that makes the most progress will receive the inheritance. The one who will have not progressed will be dominated by the other, and eliminated. This is also true on earth between nations. In Chapter 26, Jesus reveals the importance of his death and of the writings which would later serve as proof. When one of those who was with Jesus tried to defend him with a sword, he said:

'Put back your sword into its place .... Do you suppose that I cannot appeal to my father, who would at once send to my aid more than twelve legions of angels?' Matthew 26:53.

'How then could the Scriptures be fulfilled, which say that must be.'

It was in fact necessary for Jesus to die in order for the truth to be known throughout the world, so that later on, when the creators return to earth, they are not taken for usurpers or invaders. That is the purpose of the Biblical and Evangelical writings; so that the trace of their work and their presence be kept, so that they would be recognised when they return.

After his death Jesus 'resuscitates' with the help of the creators.

'Suddenly there was a violent earthquake, for an angel of the Lord came down from heaven, and drawing near, rolled back the stone, and sat upon it . . . . His face shone like lightning, his garments were white as snow.' Matthew 28:2.

The creators take care of and revive Jesus. And he said:

'Go therefore, and make disciples of all nations . . . teaching them to observe all that I have commanded you.' Matthew 28: 19-20.

The mission of Jesus was coming to an end.

'So then the Lord, after he had spoken to them, was taken up into heaven . . . .' Mark 16:19.

The creators took him away after this last important sentence: 'if they shall take up serpents: and if they drink any deadly thing, it shall not hurt them, they shall lay hands upon the sick and they shall get well.' Mark 16: 17-18.

This will happen when men will have discovered antivenom serums, and antidotes, and when they will have developed surgery, etc. This is happening now. Before returning, the creators will appear more and more frequently, in order to give more weight to their revelations, in preparation for their arrival on earth. This is what is happening right now!

'Look at the fig tree . . . when they now put forth their buds, you know that summer is near.' Luke 21:30.

When many unidentified flying objects appear, as they do now, it will mean that the time has come.

In the Acts of the Apostles, it is said once more in

Chapter 2:

'And when the days of Pentecost were drawing to a close, they were all together in one place . . . and suddenly there came a sound from heaven as of a violent wind blowing, and it filled the whole house where they were sitting . . . and there appeared to them parted tongues as of fire, which settled upon each of them . . . and they were all filled with the holy spirit and began to speak in foreign tongues . . . .' Acts 2:1 to 4.

By means of a teaching method, which was condensed into and inculcated through amplified telepathic waves, and applied in a form similar to electroshock, the creators were able to imprint the elements of other languages in the apostles' memories, so that they could spread the truth throughout the world.

In 'The Acts of the Apostles', we must take note of some appearances by the creators, the 'angels', on several occasions, particularly when they liberated Peter who had been chained by Herod.

'And behold an Angel of the Lord stood beside him, and a light shone in the room; and he struck Peter on the side and woke him, saying, 'Get up quickly'. The chains dropped . . . and the angel said to him, 'Gird thyself and put on thy sandals'. And he did so. And he said to him, 'Wrap thy cloak about thee and follow me . . . .' And he followed him out, without knowing that what was being done by the angel was real, for he thought he was having a vision.' Acts 12: 7-9.

Peter, as primitive as he was, thought he was having

a vision as his chains fell off. He did not know about the electronic laser welding torch which was being used by one of the creators. When such amazing things happen, we think we are dreaming.

This is why it is often said of people who have seen the creators, that they were having a vision or have seen them in a dream. In the same way, it is said of the people who have seen our flying saucers that they have had hallucinations. There, it is quite clearly explained that he thought he had seen it in a dream but it was in fact very real!

'And came to the iron gate that leads into the city; and this opened to them of its own accord . . . and straightaway the angel left him.' Acts of the Apostles 12:10.

Another sign that the time has come is that the people of Israel have regained their country.

'After these things I will return and will rebuild the tabernacle of David which has fallen down.' Acts of the Apostles 15:16.

Another important sentence is found in the following:

'For we are also his offspring.' Acts of the Apostles 17:28, which was said by an apostle while speaking of God.

We shall not continue to read further on in the Gospels, where there are still many more references to the creators, but of less importance. You can interpret them by yourself, to those who ask questions, in the light of the explanations I have given you up to now."

And then he left, just as before.

CHAPTER V
THE END OF THE WORLD

1946, Year 1 of the New Era

The End of the Church

The Creation of the State of Israel

The Mistakes of the Church

At the Origin of all Religions

Man: A Disease of the Universe

Evolution: A Myth

1946, Year 1 of the New Era

The next day, just as before, he returned and started to speak. "The time of the end of the world has arrived. Not the end of the world in a catastrophe destroying the earth, but the end of the world of the Church, because it has completed its mission. It did it more or less effectively. It was a work of vulgarisation, allowing the creators to be recognised when they return. As you have noticed, the Christian Church is dying. It is the end of this world because its mission has been completed, although with quite a few mistakes, because it tried for so long to deify the creators.

This deification was good up until the coming of the scientific civilisation, when a sharp turn should have been taken in their thinking, if the real truth had been kept or if they had been able to read between the lines. But too many mistakes were made. This was predicted by the creators, and the Church will collapse, being no longer of any use. The scientifically developed countries are already full of moroseness, and they have little faith left in anything. No one can believe any longer in a 'heavenly God' with a white beard, perched upon a cloud, omniscient and omnipotent which the Church wants us to believe in. Neither can they believe in delightful little guardian angels, nor in a devil with horns and hooves . . . so, no one knows what to believe. Only a few young people have understood that love is essential. You have reached the Golden Age.

Men of the earth, you fly in the heavens and carry your voices to the four corners of the earth, using radio waves, the time has come for you to know the truth. As it was written, everything is happening now that the earth has entered the Age of Aquarius. Certain people have already written on this subject, but they were not believed. 22,000 years ago, the creators decided to start their work on earth.

Everything was planned, because the movement of the galaxy implies this knowledge. The age of Pisces was the age of Christ and his fishermen, and the Age of Aquarius which follows arrived in 1946. This is the era when the people of Israel found their country again:

'And there shall be in that day, the noise of a cry from the pisces gate . . . ' Sophonias 1.

The Gate of Pisces is the passageway to the age of Aquarius . . . This is the moment when the sun rises over the earth on the day of the vernal equinox 'in' the constellation Aquarius. The loud clamour is the sound that the revelation will make. It is not by chance that you were born in 1946.

The End of the Church

This revelation will bring new hope and happiness to people who are morose because of the enlightenment it carries. It will also hasten the fall of the Church unless it understands its mistakes, and places itself at the service of the truth.

'For the terrible is brought to nought, and the scorner is consumed and all that watch for iniquity are cut off. That make man an offender for a word, and lay a snare for him that reproveth in the gate, and turn aside the just for a thing of nought.' Isaiah 29:20-21.

It is the end of people who want to make us believe in the original sin and make us feel guilty, the end of those people who lay traps for those who spread the truth at the end of Pisces and the beginning of Aquarius, trying to save the Church as it existed, ousting the just, those who speak of justice, and those who write or preach the truth. Just like the people who crucified Jesus, who were convinced they were defending what was right without trying to understand. They were frightened of being ruined and destroyed at the passing into the Era of Pisces.

'The eyes of them that see shall not be dim, and the ears of them that hear shall hearken diligently . . . the fool shall no more be called prince; neither shall the deceitful be called great.'

'For the fool will speak foolish things, and his heart will work iniquity, to practice hypocrisy, and speak of Yahwe deceitfully, and to make empty the soul of the hungry, and take away drink from the thirsty . . . The villain's ways are villainous, and he devises infamous plans to ruin the poor with his lies, and deny justice to the needy. But the man of noble mind forms noble designs and stands firm in his nobility.' Isaiah 32.

Everyone will then understand, 'the eyes of those that see shall not be dim'. It is the Church who addresses Yahwe in aberrant ways, and leaves empty the souls of those who are hungry for the truth; it is the Church who makes plans to destroy the poor, so that those who are unable to understand, or who dare not understand, will remain faithful to it through the fear of sin, of excommunication or of other nonsense. In the meantime, the pauper states his case, while those who lack the intelligence to seize the truth, stand up for the Church's lies, on the Church's advice. But the one who is noble, the one who will cry out the truth loudly, projects noble acts, even if he lives without the assent of men's agonising Church.

'Do you not know, have you not heard, were you not told long ago, have you not perceived ever since the world began? Do you not understand the foundation of the earth?' Isaiah 40.

'Here is my servant, whom I uphold, my chosen one in whom I delight, I have bestowed my spirit upon him, and he will make justice shine on the nations.' Isaiah 42.

You are the one who will spread the truth throughout the world, this truth which has been revealed to you over the past few days.

'He will not break a bruised reed, or snuff out a smouldering wick.' Isaiah 42.

You will not be able to destroy the Church and its lies completely, but eventually it will fade out by itself. This extinction has already been going on for some time. 'The wick is weakening' It has accomplished its mission, and it is time for it to disappear. It has made mistakes and has enriched itself at the expense of the truth, without trying to interpret it in a clear enough way for men of this era. But don't be too hard on it, for it has spread the word of the Bible, a witness to the truth, throughout the world. But its mistakes were great, particularly that of inserting too much of the supernatural into the truth, and that of wrongly translating the 'Biblical writings' by replacing the term 'Elohim' which designates the creators, with God, a singular term, whereas Elohim in Hebrew is the plural of Eloha, transforming the creators in this way into a single incomprehensible God. Another mistake was to make people adore a wooden cross in memory of Jesus Christ. A cross is not the Christ. A piece of wood in the shape of a cross means nothing.

'Such a man will not use his reason, he has neither the wit nor the sense to say: Half of it I have burnt, yes, and use its embers to bake bread, I have roasted meat on them too and eaten it; but the rest of it I turn into this abominable thing and so I am worshipping a log of wood.' Isaiah 44.

The Creation of the State of Israel

The return of the Jews to Israel, as it was written, is a sign of the Golden Age.

'I will bring your children from the east and gather you all from the west. I will say to the north: give them up, and to the south: do not hold them back. Bring my sons and daughters from afar, bring them from the ends of the earth; bring every one who is called by my name. All whom I have created whom I have formed, all whom I have made for my glory.' Isaiah 43.

This is indeed the creation of the State of Israel welcoming Jews from the North and from the South. The Bible, preserved by the Jewish people, bears witness to the coming of the creators as it is written:

'You are my witnesses.'

'Lead out those who have eyes but are blind, who have ears but are deaf. Let all the nations be gathered together and the people assembled. Which of them proclaimed to us the former things and foretold this? Let them bring in their witnesses to prove that they were right, so that others may hear and say "it is true".'

'You are my witnesses, saith Yahwe, and my servant whom I have chosen: That you may know and believe me, and understand that I am he:... You are my witnesses, declares the Lord, that I am God, yes and from ancient days I am one and the same.' Isaiah 43.

'You are my witnesses', that's quite explicit, isn't it? . . . and I can tell you again on this day: 'from ancient days I am one, and the same.' thanks to the witness, that you hold in your hand, the Bible.

'For a small moment I have forsaken thee; but with great mercies will I gather thee.' Isaiah 54.

The Jewish people have in fact regained their country after having participated in the safeguarding of the truth.

The time when men will cure illnesses by scientific means is predicted:

'There shall be no more thence an infant of days,

nor an old man that hath not filled his days.' Isaiah 65.

Medicine helps men triumph over illnesses and especially over infant mortality.

'In the lips of him that hath understanding, wisdom is found; but a rod is for the back of him that is void of understanding.' Proverbs 10.

The Mistakes of the Church

The Church was wrong in accusing man of being guilty and making him pray without understanding.

'But when you pray, use not vain repetitions, as the heathen do: for they think that they shall be heard for their much speaking.' Matthew 6.

And yet it is written in the Gospel. The Church has also enriched itself too much, although it was written:

'No man can serve two masters: for either he will hate the one, and love the other; or else he will hold to the one, and despise the other. You cannot serve God and Mammon.(1) Lay not up for yourselves treasure upon earth.' Matthew 6.

'Provide neither gold, nor silver, not brass in your purses, nor scrip for your journey, neither two coats, neither shoes, not yet staves.' Matthew 10.

With their stupid rules and meatless Fridays, they were not obeying their own Gospels:

'Not that which goeth into the mouth defileth a

(1) Mammon means 'wealth' in Aramean.

man; but that which cometh out of the mouth, this defileth a man.' Matthew 15.

How dare they, these men who are nothing but men, indulge themselves in fortunes and luxuries of the Vatican, when the Gospels tell them to possess 'neither gold, nor silver', not even a spare coat. How dare they preach goodness?

'Then said Jesus unto his disciples, verily I say unto you, that a rich man shall hardly enter into the Kingdom of Heaven.' Matthew 19.

'Then make up heavy packs and pile them on men's shoulders; but they themselves will not move them with one of their fingers. But all their works they do for to be seen of men . . . and love the upper-most rooms at feasts . . . and greetings in the markets . . . . For you have one master, and you are all brothers. Do not call any man on earth 'father', for you have one father, and he is in heaven. Nor must you be called 'teacher'; you have one teacher, the Christ. But the greatest among you must be your servant.' Matthew 23.

And yet it is written in their Gospels. How dare the Church burden men with their so called sins, which are only different concepts of morality and ways of life, speak of goodness while living in opulence in the Vatican while people are dying of hunger, and seek invitations and honours while preaching humility; how dare they ask the people to call them father, your eminence, or your holiness, when their Gospels forbid it? If tomorrow the Pope took to the road as a pauper the Church would relive, but with a totally different humanitarian goal than that which it had up to now, that is to say, the diffusion of what must serve as proof for today. That mission is finished, but the Church could reorientate itself in the direction of goodness by helping those who are unhappy, by helping to spread the real truth of those writings which, until now, have been deformed or kept secret. In this way, the magnanimity of many clergymen could be fulfilled. For that to happen, the Vatican should set an example by selling all its treasures to help finance the underdeveloped countries, and by going there to help men to progress, with their own bare hands, and not just with 'The good word'. Matthew 23.

It is inadmissible that there be different categories of marriages, and more particularly of burials, according to a man's fortune. This is another of the Church's mistakes. But the time has come.

At the Origin of all Religions

It is not only in the Bible and the Gospels that there are traces of the truth; testimonies are found in practically every religion. 'The Cabbala' especially is one of the richest in testimonies, but it would not have been easy for you to find one. But if one day you can find a copy, then you will be able to see that there are a great number of allusions to us. Especially a description in the Canticle of Canticles (5) which speaks of the creators' planet and of the distance which separates it from the earth. It is said that the 'height of the creator' is of 236,000 'parasangs' and that the 'height of his heels' is of 30 million 'parasangs'. The parasang is a unit of measure just like the parsec, which signifies the distance that light can travel in one second, which is about 300,000 kilometres. Our planet is at 30 million parasangs, or at least nine thousand billion kilometres, just a little less than light year.

By moving at the speed of light, or 300,000 kilometres per second, it would take you almost one year to reach our planet. With your present day rockets, which only move at 40,000 kilometres per hour, it would then take you about 90,000 years before reaching our planet. So you can see that we have nothing to fear for the time being. We have the means to go to the earth from our planet in less than two months, with a propulsion method using the atom, enabling us to move at the speed of rays that are seven times faster than the speed of light. Those rays 'carry' us. So in order to be 'carried' by them, we must leave the optical window, which is the spectrum of rays detected by the eyes, permitting us to be attuned to the carrying beam. That is why observers from the earth have described our spaceships as becoming bright, a very brilliant white, then blue, and finally disappearing.

It is quite obvious that when a spaceship goes beyond the speed of light it 'disappears' and is no longer visible to the naked eye. This is the height of the creators' 'heels', the distance at which his heels rest on a planet. The creators' planet is far from his Sun by 236,000 parasangs, or seventy billion, eight hundred thousand kilometres, which is the creators' height in relation to his Sun, a large star.

'The Cabbala' is the book closest to the truth, but almost all religious books make allusions to us more or less clearly, especially in the countries in which the creators had their bases: in Cordillera des Los Andes, in the Himalayas, in Greece, where the Mythology also contains important testimonies, in the Buddhist and Islamic religions, the Mormons. It would take pages and pages to name all the religions and sects that testify in a more or less obscure way to our work.

Man: A Disease of the Universe

There, now you know the truth. You must write it down and make it known throughout the world. If men of the earth want us to make them benefit from our knowledge, by making them gain 25,000 years of scientific knowledge, they have to show us that they want to meet us, and especially that they have earned it, so that this can be done without any danger to us. If we give our knowledge to humans, we have to be sure they will make good use of it. Our observations of the past years have not shown us that wisdom rules the earth. Certainly there has been progress, but some men still die of hunger, and a warlike spirit still exists throughout the world. We know that our arrival could improve many things and unite the nations, but we have to feel that people really want to see us, and that they are truly preparing to be unified.

We also have to feel that they really want to see us arrive, knowing who we really are, and what is the true meaning of our arrival. Several times human war planes have tried to chase ours, taking them in fact for enemies. You must tell them who we are, so that we can dare show ourselves without the risk of either getting hurt or killed, which is not the case at present, and without risking a dangerous and murderous panic. Some researchers want to contact us by radio, but we don't want to answer because in this way they could locate our planet. On the other hand, the time of transmission would be too long, and our broadcasting system uses waves that your technology cannot perceive, because you have not yet discovered them. They are seven times faster than radioelectric waves, and we are experimenting with new waves that are one and a half times faster than the latter. Progress continues, and your own research continues, for the purpose of understanding and coming in contact with the large being of whom we are a part, and on whose atoms we are parasites, these atoms being the planets and the stars.

In fact, we have been able to discover in the infinitely small, intelligent living beings who live on particles that are planets and suns to them, asking the same questions as we are. Man is a 'disease' of the gigantic being of whom the planets and the stars are the atoms. In both directions there is Infinity. But the important thing is to make sure that our 'disease', humanity, continues to exist and that it never dies. We did not know while we were creating you, that we were accomplishing a secondary mission, 'written' in us, thus repeating what had been done for us. We have discovered through our creation, and from its evolution, our own origins. For we were also created by other men who have disappeared. Their world was surely disintegrated, but thanks to them, we were able to continue in their steps and create you. We may disappear one day, but by then you will have taken our place and our roles. So you are the link of a precious human continuity. Other worlds exist and humanity is certainly developing in other parts of the Universe. But in this part, our world is the only one to have created, and that is important because from each world could come innumerable children, precious for continuity. This allows us to hope that one day man will no longer be in danger of disappearing completely. But we are not sure that man can ever stabilise himself as a multitude. The chain has always continued, and the equilibrium of the big body in which we are a sickness, a parasite, does not want us to develop too much because we might cause a catastrophe that would result in at best a recession, at worst, complete destruction. Just like in a healthy body, a few germs can live without danger, but if they develop into large quantities, they bring on a disease that troubles the organism, which reacts either naturally or with the help of medication destroying the responsible germs. The important thing is apparently to create enough worlds so that humanity does not extinguish itself, and especially to make sure that the equilibrium is not broken, by transferring our efforts to search for the improvement of the happiness of those who exist. It is in this area that we can help you tremendously.

Evolution: A Myth

Incidentally, you must dissipate from your mind all doubts about evolution. Your scientists who have elaborated the theory of evolution are not completely wrong in saying that man descends from the monkey and the monkey from the fish, etc. In reality the first living organism created on Earth was unicellular, and afterwards it produced more complicated beings. But not by chance. When we came to create life on earth, we started by making very simple creations, and then improved our techniques of environmental adaptation. Next we made fishes, the batrachians, the mammals, the birds, the primates, and finally man, who is only an improved model of the monkey, to which we added that which makes us men.

We made him in our image, as it is written in the Biblical Genesis. You could have realised by yourself that an accidental evolution would have little chance of producing such a large variety of forms of life, of birds' colours, of their amorous demonstrations, of the shape of the horns of certain antelope. What natural need could lead antelopes or certain wild goats to have curled horns? Or the birds to have blue or red feathers, and what about exotic fish?

That's the work of our 'artists'. Do not forget artists when you yourself create life. Imagine a world where artists do not exist, no music, films, paintings, or sculptures, etc. Life would be very boring and animals very ugly if their bodies corresponded only to their needs and functions. The evolution of the forms of life on earth is the evolution of the techniques of creation and the sophistication of the brilliant work realised by the creators which eventually led to the creation of a being similar to them. You can find human prehistoric skulls which are the first human prototypes which were replaced each time by others much more evolved, right until the type which is the exact replica of the creators, who were afraid to create a being who could be far superior to them, although some were tempted to.

If we were sure that they would never turn against their creators to dominate them or to destroy them, which is what happened between the different human races successively created on earth, instead of loving them as fathers, the temptation would be great to create an improved humankind. This is possible, but what an enormous risk! Some creators are even afraid that men from earth may be slightly superior to their fathers: 'Satan' is one of those who has always thought, and still thinks, that men from earth are a danger to our planet, because they are a little too intelligent. But the majority among us think that you will prove to us that you love us, and that you will never try to harm us. That is the least we expect before coming to help you. It is even possible that at each creation of man by man, a small improvement is realised, a true evolution of the human race, but

slowly, so that the creators do not feel in danger of being confronted with their creation, permitting progress to be made even faster. Although we do not think that we can at present give you our scientific knowledge, we do think that we can give you, without any danger, our political and humanitarian knowledge. Although this will not threaten your planet, it will permit you to be happier on earth, and thanks to this happiness, you will progress faster. That will help you to show us more rapidly that you deserve our help and our inheritance, in order to achieve an intergalactic level of civilisation.

Otherwise, if man's aggressiveness does not calm down, if peace does not become the only goal, and if people are allowed to encourage war by producing firearms, war-like atomic experiments, or the armies are allowed to continue to exist, or to stay in power, or to take over, then we will stop them from becoming a danger to us, and it would be another 'Sodom and Gomorrah'. How could we not fear men from earth, when they attack their own, we who are from another world and slightly different?

You, Claude Vorilhon, you will spread the truth under your present name which you will replace progressively with 'RAEL', which means literally 'light of God', and if we translate more accurately 'light of the Elohim' or 'Ambassador of the Elohim', because you will be our ambassador on earth, and we will come officially only to your Embassy. Rael can simply be translated by 'messenger'.

And it is by telepathy that we have made you call

your son Ramuel, which means 'the son of the one who brings light' because he is truly the son of our messenger, of our ambassador."

And he left, just like the other mornings.

CHAPTER VI
THE NEW COMMANDMENTS

Geniocracy

Humanitarianism

World Government

Your Mission

Geniocracy

I met him again the next day and he spoke.

"First of all, let's look at the political and economical aspects.

'What kind of men allow humanity to progress? The geniuses. Your world must take advantage of the geniuses, and allow them to run the earth. You have successively had in power the 'brutes' who were superior to others by their muscular strength, the rich, who had the money to have 'brutes' at their service, and the politicians who have trapped the people of the democratic countries with their own hopes, not to mention the military men who have based their achievements on a rational organisation of brutality. The only type of men who have never been placed in power are the ones who make humanity progress. Whether they discover the wheel, gunpowder, the motor engine or the atom, the genius has always allowed the less intelligent men in power to benefit from his inventions, although they often used the genius' peaceful inventions for murderous ends. This must change!

In order for this to happen, elections must be abolished and also the votes which are completely unadapted in their present form to suit the evolution of humanity. Each person is a useful cell of a huge body which is called humanity. The cell of the foot should not determine whether the hand should take an object or not. It is the brain which must decide, and if that object is good, the cell of the foot will benefit from it. The foot is not required to vote since it is designed just to move the body, of which the brain is a part, forwards and it is not capable of judging if what the hand takes is good or not. Votes are positive only when there is equality of knowledge and intellectual level. Copernicus was condemned by a majority of incapable people, because he was the only one to have a sufficiently high level of understanding.

And yet the earth is not the centre of the world, as the Church believed. It really revolved around the Sun.

When the first car came out, had we asked everyone to vote to know if the cars were to be authorised or not, the people who knew nothing about cars, and did not care, would have responded negatively, and you would still be riding a horse and buggy. How do you change all of that?

Now you have psychologists who are capable of creating tests to evaluate the intelligence and the adaptation of each individual. Right from infancy on, those tests must be systematically applied in order to define the orientation of the subject's studies, and when the individual reaches an age where he becomes responsible, we may finally define his intellectual coefficient, which will be marked on his identity card or voter's card. Only those who have an intellectual coefficient of at least 50% above the average will be eligible for a public post, and those who will be able to vote will have an intellectual coefficient of at least

10% above the average. Many of your present-day politicians would not be able to perform their functions if this testing existed today. This is a totally democratic system. There are some engineers whose intelligence is lower than the average, but who have a memory, and who have obtained quite a few degrees because of this. There are some workers or peasants who are not specialised at all, but who have an intelligence of over 50% above the average. What is presently unacceptable is that the voice of one whom you vulgarly call 'stupid' is worth as much as that of the genius who has thought maturely about the way he is going to vote.

In some small cities, the elections are won by the one who buys people the largest number of drinks . . . not by the one whose project seems to be the most interesting.

Therefore, as a start, the right to vote is reserved for the intellectual elite, whose brains are more apt to think and to find solutions to problems. This does not necessarily mean those who have done the most studying. You must place the genius in power, and you may call that Geniocracy.

Humanitarianism

Second point: Your world is paralysed by profit, and communism has not succeeded in giving men enough rewards to sufficiently motivate him and make him want to progress. You are all born equal; this is also written in the Bible. The government should ensure that people are born with about the same fortune. It is inadmissible that unintelligent children should live in luxury thanks to the fortunes that their fathers have gathered, while geniuses die of hunger, and do any menial chore just to be able to eat, forsaking in this way occupations where they could have made discoveries benefiting all humanity. To avoid this, owning property must be eliminated without establishing communism.

This world is not yours; that also is written in the Bible. You are only tenants. Thus, all goods should be rented for forty-nine years. This eliminates the injustice of inheritance. Your inheritance and that of your children, is the whole world, if you know how to organise yourselves to make it pleasant. This political orientation of humanity is not communism: its preoccupation is the future of humanity. If you want to give a name to it, call it Humanitarianism.

Take for example: a man who has finished his studies at the age of twenty-one, wants to work, chooses a profession and earns a certain amount of money. If he wants to find a place to live, while his parents are still alive, he 'buys' a house, but of course he really is renting a house or an apartment for forty-nine years from the State that constructed it. If the house is estimated at one hundred thousand francs, he will pay that amount in monthly payments for forty-nine years. At seventy (21 plus 49), he will have paid for his house and he will live there until his death, without ever paying again.

After his death, the house will go back to the State,

which must let the children benefit from it freely if there are any. Supposing there is one child, then he will live freely all his life in his father's house. At his death, his child will also benefit from the family house, and this goes on and on. Inheritance must be completely abolished except for the family house. This does not prevent each person from being rewarded for his merits. Let's take another example. A man has two children. One is a good worker and the other is lazy. At the age of twenty-one, they both decide to go their separate ways. They each rent a house worth one hundred thousand francs. The worker will rapidly earn more money than the lazy one. He will then be able to rent a house worth twice as much as the first one. If he has the means, he will even be able to rent both houses, one being a country house. He will also be able, if his savings are fruitful, to build a house and rent it for forty-nine years, thereby receiving the money in exchange. But at his death, everything will go to the community, except for the family house, which will go to his children.

Thus, a man can make a fortune for himself, depending on his own merits, but not for his children. To each his own merits. It is the same thing for commercial and industrial enterprises. If a person creates a business, it is then his own during all his life, and he can rent it out, but never for more than forty-nine years. The same goes for farmers, they can rent land and cultivate it for 49 years, but after that it all goes back to the State, which will be able to rent it out again for forty-nine years. The children can also rent it for forty-nine years. It must be this way for all goods that remain exploitable, and as for the value of the things, nothing changes. Everything that is of value such as shares, gold, enterprises, cash, or buildings are all owned by the community, but may be rented for forty-nine years by those who have acquired the means by their own merits and labour. In this way, a man having made his fortune around the age of forty will be able to construct houses, rent them as apartments for forty-nine years, and enjoy that money until he dies. Afterwards, the money which comes from those rents will go back to the community. This humanitarianism is already prescribed in the Bible: 'You shall count seven sabbaths of years, that is seven times seven years, forty-nine years.'

'When you sell or buy land amongst yourselves, neither party shall drive a hard bargain. You shall pay your fellow countryman according to the number of years since the jubilee, and he shall sell to you according to the number of annual crops. The more years are to run, the higher the price, the fewer the years, the lower the price, because he is selling you a series of crops . . . .'

'No land shall be sold outright, because the land is mine, and you are coming into it as aliens and settlers.' Leviticus 25.

If the genius is admitted to power, he will understand the usefulness of those reforms. You must also have all the nations of the earth unite to form only one government.

World Government

The thing that would help you to achieve this is the creation of a new world-wide currency and a common language. Auvergnat is no longer spoken in Clermont-Ferrand, and very soon French will no longer be spoken in Paris, nor English in London, nor German in Frankfurt. Your scientists and linguistic specialists must unite and work to create a new language inspired by all the languages and made obligatory in all the schools of the whole world, as a second language. It is the same thing with currency. The world-wide value can be neither the franc nor the dollar nor the yen, but a new currency created for the needs of the whole earth, without people asking themselves why another currency has been chosen over their own.

Finally, the necessary detonator to such union is the suppression of military draft, which only teaches aggressiveness to young men, and the assigning of professional military men to the service of public order. This must occur in all countries at the same time as an indispensable pledge of security.

Your Mission

As I have already told you, we know that our official arrival would accelerate many things. But we will wait until we see that men really want us to come, that they love us and respect us like the fathers that we are . . . . That our machines won't be threatened by your destructive warrior forces.

To achieve this, cry out throughout the world that you have met me and repeat what I have said to you. Wise people will listen to you. A lot of people will take you for a madman or a visionary, but I have already explained what to think of the foolish majorities.

You know the truth, and we will stay in contact with you by telepathy, to give you confidence and to give you additional information if we think it necessary. What we want is to see if there are enough wise people on earth. If there are enough people who follow us, then we will come back openly. Where? At the place you will have prepared for our arrival.

Have a residence built in a pleasant country with a mild climate with seven rooms always ready to receive guests, each with a separate bathroom, a conference room able to receive at least twenty-one people, one swimming pool and a dining room being able to receive twenty-one people. That residence should be constructed in the centre of a park. The residence should be protected from curious onlookers. The park should be entirely surrounded by walls, to prevent anyone from seeing the residence and the swimming pool. The residence should be situated at a distance of at least one thousand metres from the wall around the park. It will have a maximum of two stories and be concealed from the outskirts of the wall by a sheet of vegetation.

Two entrances will be installed in the surrounding wall, one in the south and the other one on the northern side. The residence will also have two entrances. There will be a terrace on the roof of the residence where a craft of twelve metres in diameter may land. And an access from that terrace to the interior is indispenable. The aerial space situated over and surrounding the residence should not be under direct military or radar surveillance. You will try to obtain that the land where this residence is established (if possible, larger than prescribed) be considered neutral territory by other nations, and by the nation in which it is located, by virtue of it being our embassy on earth. You may live with your wife and your children in the residence which will be under your direction, and you will be able to have servants and guests of your choosing. However, the part containing the seven rooms should be directly under the terrace and separated by a thick metal door, permanently closed, which should be able to be locked from the interior, to separate it from the section used by men. An aseptic chamber should be built at the entrance of the conference room.

The financing of this realisation will be possible, thanks to the help you will obtain from those who believe in you, and therefore, in us, who will be wise and intelligent. They will be rewarded when we come. Keep a record therefore of those who contribute financially to this realisation, however modest their contribution, for the edification or upkeep of the residence, and throughout the world in each nation take a responsible person who will spread the truth, and permit people to unite themselves in spreading it.

On a mountain near the residence, gather together once a year people from all over the world, who wish us to come, after having gained knowledge of these writings.

Have the largest number possible, and make them think intensely about us, and hope for our coming. When there are enough of them and when they wish for our coming intensely enough without any religious mysticism, as responsible people respecting their creators, we will come openly and give our scientific knowledge as our heritage to all peoples of the earth. If the warlike temperaments are reduced to total powerlessness in the whole world, this will happen. If the love of life and humanity for us, and therefore for itself, is strong enough, yes we will come openly. We will wait. And if humans remain aggressive and progress in a manner which is dangerous for other worlds, then we will destroy that civilisation and locations storing their scientific wealth, and it will be another 'Sodom and Gomorrah' until humanity is morally worthy of its scientific level.

The future of man is in his own hands, and the truth is in yours. Spread it throughout the world and do not be discouraged. We will never help you openly in any way that would give proof to the sceptics, since scepticism often goes together with aggressiveness. The intelligent ones will believe you since what you will say contains nothing mystical. It is important to us that they believe you without any material proof. This proves to us more than anything else that they are intelligent and so, worthy to receive from us the scientific knowledge.

Now, go, you will not be forgotten if you succeed during your life on earth, and even after, if we have to wait for your descendants to come, for we can scientifically make you live again, just as we can all those who will have led people on the path of human genius with the creators' love as guides, on the condition that their remains be kept in coffins.

Our only help will be to appear, more and more frequently from now on in order to make people aware of the problem, and to make them wish to learn more about the truth that you are transmitting to them. Progressively, thanks to our increased number of appearances, public opinion will be sensitised, and our presence will no longer trigger stupid adoration, but instead within the populations, a deep desire to come in contact with us.

You will call your movement the 'Madech'(1) the movement for the welcoming of the Elohim, Creators of humanity, which carries in its initials a message, 'Moses has preceded Elijah and the Christ'. In French:

M : mouvement pour (movement for)
A : l'accueil (the welcoming)
D : des (of the)
E : Elohim
C : créateurs de (creators of)
H : l'humanité (humanity)
'Moise a devance Elie et le Christ' "

(1) In 1975, with the authorisation of the Elohim, the name of the Movement was changed to the 'Raelian Movement'.

CHAPTER VII
THE ELOHIM

Atomic Bombs

Overpopulation

The Secret of Eternity

Chemical Education

Raelian Movement

Atomic Bombs

"Before we leave each other for the last time, do you have any questions to ask me?"

"You have described the vision of Ezekiel as men equipped with pressurised suits, and told me that the atmosphere of your planet was not the same as the atmosphere on the earth. Why do you not wear a pressurised suit now?"

"Because we have also progressed scientifically, and now we can do without them. My face seems to be in the open air, but in reality it is protected by an invisible shield composed of repellent rays inside of which I breathe air different from yours. These rays let the waves pass, but not the air molecules. You can compare that to the emission of bubbles which are made inside of your ports, keeping the fuel residues from coming out."

"Are atomic bombs a danger for humanity?"

"Yes, a great danger. But this will enable us, if we have to, to easily destory that civilisation if men cannot become wise, maybe they will destroy themselves. If they do not, and become threatening for us, we will only have to destroy their stocks of bombs without sending offensive weapons against them. We could do this by rays, or by telepathy, in such a way that one of the great powers becomes the 'aggressor', which would release automatically a fatal retaliation.

If men do not want to be exposed to that danger any longer, they only have to take the atomic weapons away from the military. Their power, applied gently, would enable countries which lack energy to make great steps forward. It would be urgent for you to stop the nuclear tests, because you do not know what you are exposing yourselves to. However, if men continue to play with atomic weapons, it will simplify things for us, in case we have to reduce them to silence."

"Do you have any women on your planet?"

"Yes, it is mentioned in the Bible, and I made you note the article mentioned."

"And children also?"

"Yes, we can have children exactly like you."

Overpopulation

"But you have told me you were immortal in some way. How do you struggle against overpopulation?"

"In fact, that problem will present itself very rapidly on earth. To resolve it, and you should resolve it now, because you are sufficiently numerous, you must develop contraception, and you will have to make strict laws authorising women to have only two children.

If two equals two, the population will arrive at a point where it will no longer increase. We will observe how you will pull through this, also. It is another proof of intelligence to see if you have earned our heritage. I give you the solution of your present problem, for you who only live on an average, seventy-five years of age. For us, the problem is indeed different. We are not eternal. We can live ten times longer than you, thanks to a small surgical intervention, the Biblical 'tree of life'. We have children, and we observe the rules which I have just explained: two parents, two children, which keeps our population constant."

"How many of you are there?"

"We are about seven billion."

"We have met on six consecutive days, and each time you went back to your planet?"

"No, I returned to an intergalactic ship which we use as a base and which stays constantly close to earth."

"How many are you on that vessel?"

"Seven, and on our planet there are seven provinces. Each has a representative on that vessel. If we add two who are responsible for the vessel, there are permanently nine of us."

"If the men of the earth do exactly as you wish what will happen?"

"We will officially come to the residence which you will have prepared, and we will ask you to have the official representatives of the most important countries of humanity come, in order to obtain the total unification of the people of the earth. If everything goes well, we will allow humanity to progressively benefit from our scientific advance. Depending on the use that will be made of it, we will see if we can give men all our knowledge, and then let you enter the intergalactic era with our 25,000 years scientific advance as your inheritance."

"Are you the only world to have attained this

scientific level?"

"In this region of the Universe, yes. There is an infinite number of worlds inhabited by beings of the humanoid type, whose scientific level is lower than ours, even though greatly higher than yours. The thing that makes us fearful of disappearing is that we have not found any planet having a civilisation as highly evolved as ours. We have economic relationships with many other planets, on which life has been created by other men who must have had a scientific level equal to ours, as their religious writings prove to us. Unfortunately, we have been unable to find the creative civilisations of the closest of those worlds, but perhaps we will find some farther on, as we continue to search the universe each time further away. In most cases their planet approached the sun too closely, and life became impossible, or their sun exploded, or has become too cold. Although we have not noticed anything abnormal presently in our system, all of this makes us fear the worst."

"Is there no religion where you live?"

"Our only religion is human genius. We believe only in that, and we particularly love the memory of our own creators, whom we never saw again, and whose world we have never been able to find. They must have disappeared. They had taken the precaution of putting a huge spaceship in orbit around our planet, containing all their knowledge, which landed automatically on our planet when their world was destroyed.

Thanks to them, we have taken on the torch. This

torch we would like to see taken up by the earth people."

"And if your planet was destroyed?"

"In case our world was destroyed, the same arrangement has been foreseen, so that you would automatically inherit our knowledge."

The Secret of Eternity

"You live ten times longer than us?"

"Our body lives on an average ten times longer than yours, like the first men of the Bible - between 750 and 1,200 years. But our mind, our true self, can be truly immortal. I have already explained to you that, starting with any cell of the body, we can recreate the whole being with new living matter. When we are in full possession of our abilities, and our brain is at its maximum efficiency and knowledge, we remove surgically a tiny part of the body, which is conserved. When we die, from a minute particle of our body which had already been conserved, we fully recreate the body, as it was at that time. I say as it was at that time, meaning with all its scientific knowledge, and of course, its personality. But the body is made up from new elements, and has the possibility of living one thousand of your years. And so on eternally. But, so as to limit the growth of the population, only geniuses have the right to eternity. All the men of our planet have a cell sample taken at a certain age, hoping that they will be chosen for recreation after their death. Not only do they hope for it, but they try to deserve this resurrection during their life. Once they have died, a grand council of the eternals assembles to judge, in a 'last judgement' which of those who died during the year deserves living another life. During three existances, the eternal is on a probation period, and at the end of these three lives, the council of the eternals reunites to judge, in the light of the work of each person, to determine if he is worthy of joining the council of the eternals as a perpetual member. From the moment that a person wishes to live again, he or she no longer has the right to have children. This of course does not prevent love. This helps us to understand why the scientists, who were in the council of the eternals, wished to create lives on other planets. They transferred their procreative instincts onto other planets."

"What do you call yourselves?"

"If you wish to give us a name, even though we call ourselves men and women in our language, you may call us the 'Elohim' since we came from the sky."

"What language do you speak on your planet?"

"Our official language closely resembles ancient Hebrew."

"Each day we have talked here, are you not afraid that other people might surprise us?"

"An automatic system would have warned me immediately of the approach of other men inside a dangerous radius, by air or by land."

"What is your lifestyle and your work where you live?"

"Most of our work is intellectual, as our scientific

level allows us to use robots for everything. We only work when we feel the inclination to, and then only with our brain. Only the artists and the sportsmen 'work' with their bodies, and only because they have chosen to.

Our highly evolved atomic energy is almost inexhaustible, mainly because we have discovered a means of utilising the atom in a closed circuit, and solar energy. We have many other sources of energy, and we do not necessarily use uranium in our atomic reactors, but many other simple and harmless materials."

"But if you live so long, and do not work, do you not get bored?"

"No, never, because we always do the things we like to do, and especially making love. We find our women very beautiful, and take full advantage of this fact."

"Does marriage exist?"

"No! Men and women are both free. Couples exist. Those who have chosen to live as such may do so, but they may have their freedom whenever they wish it. We all love one another. Jealousy does not exist, since everyone can have everything, and property is nonexistent. There is no criminality where we live, thus no prisons and no police. However, there are many doctors, and regular medical visits for the mind. Those who reveal the slightest lack of psychological balance that could possibly cause acts contrary to the liberty of each individual, or to the lives of others, are immediately submitted to treatment, so as to bring them back to normal."

"Can you describe the average man's day where you live?"

"In the morning he gets up, bathes, for there are swimming pools everywhere we live. He has breakfast, and then does what he feels like doing. Everybody 'works' but only because they feel like working, as there is no money where we live. Thus, those who 'work' always do it well, since it is by vocation. Only the eternals have precise missions, as for example, supervising the electronic brains and computers used for vital problems such as energy, food, and organisation, etc. Of the seven billion inhabitants, there are only seven hundred eternals, and they live entirely apart from the others. They have the priviledge of being eternal, but have the task of taking care of everything for the others, who are not obliged to work.

To these seven hundred eternals we must add two hundred and ten probationers (about seventy each year, that is to say, ten from each province). Of the seven billion inhabitants, there are only about forty million children. It is only when they become of age (between 18 and 21 years, depending on the subject) that the children undergo an operation which gives them a life-span of more than seven hundred and fifty years. From then on, they too may have children. This enables the oldest of our normal inhabitants to know their descendants up to fifty generations. Out of seven billion inhabitants, there are only about one million inactive people, and almost all of them are under treatment for psychological disorders. They are treated by our doctors during a period of six months.

Most people are interested in the arts, and they paint, sculpt, play music, write, produce films, and participate in sports, etc. We have a very leisurely civilisation in the full sense of the word. Our cities have an average population of about five hundred thousand people spread over a very small area. A city is actually a huge house situated on a high place, inside of which people can sleep, love, and do just what they please. These 'city houses' are about one kilometre in length and height, and are traversed in all directions by collective waves used for travel. You tie on a belt, and then place yourself in a wave-current which transports you very rapidly to wherever you wish to go.

The cities are sort of cubic in shape, so as not to 'eat up' the countryside as is the case where you live. Indeed, one of your cities with say a 500,000 population covers a surface area twenty times greater than ours. The result is that when you want to go in the country, you have to travel many hours, whereas in our case we are there in only ten seconds. An entire city is conceived by the same architect, so that it will be pleasing to the eye, and will harmonise perfectly with the scenery surrounding it."

"But, don't the people who have nothing to do get bored?"

"No, because we provide them with numerous activities. The individual's true values are recognised, and everyone wants to show he has values. Whether it be in art, in science or in sports, each wants to shine in order to become eternal, or simply to be admired by the community, or . . . by a woman. Some people like to take risks, and to deprive them of the risk of dying would take away their joy of living, and that is why dangerous sports are very popular.

We can bring back to life any injured person, but those who practice these sports may only do so if they state in writing, that they agree not to be taken care of if they die during their sporting activities. We have a kind of atomic automobile race that would fascinate you, and more brutal activities like boxing, and even more brutal, a kind of rugby game which is played in the nude, and where everything is permitted - boxing, wrestling, etc. All this may seem barbaric to you, but do not forget that all extremes must be balanced to avoid breakdowns.

An extremely sophisticated civilisation should have primitive counter balances. If our people did not have their idols in their favourite sport, they would have only one wish left, to die.

The life of another must be respected, but their wish to die, or to play with death, must also be respected, within a framework of well defined specialities. Where we live there are contests each year in all the branches of activities, one of which is a worldwide contest, permitting us to decide on the best of them for eternity. Everyone lives only for that. Each year, whether it be in painting, literature, biology, medicine, or in any other speciality where the human brain can express itself, a contest takes place in every province with a vote of the eternals of that province.

The 'champions' are regrouped in the capital, to be submitted to the vote of a jury of eternals, which designates the champions of champions. Those are presented to the council of the eternals, and the latter choose those who are worthy of becoming eternal probationers.

This is the goal - this is everyone's ideal. Distractions may take a primitive aspect when the supreme goal is so high."

"Does this mean that the eternals have a totally different way of life than the other inhabitants?"

"Oh yes! They live apart in cities reserved for them, where they assemble regularly to make decisions."

"How old are the oldest ones?"

"The oldest, the president of the council of the eternals, is twenty-five thousand years old, and you see him in front of you. I have inhabited twenty-five bodies up to this day, and I was the first one on whom this experiment was realised. That is why I am the president of the eternals. I myself directed the creation of life on earth."

"Then your knowledge must be incommensurable?"

"Yes, I have accumulated quite a lot of knowledge, but I will not be able to accumulate much more. It is in this way that man on earth may be superior to us, because the volume of the part of his brain which accumulates information, the memory, is larger. Men on earth will be able to accumulate more knowledge than us, and therefore will advance further scientifically, if they have the means. This is what frightens those who oppose the council of the eternals. Men from earth can progress faster than us, if nothing stops them."

Chemical Education

"But the knowledge that the students must accumulate must be enormous, and take a very long time?"

"No, thanks to an important scientific discovery, which in fact your scientists are beginning to discover, we can teach a student his lessons surgically.

Your scientists have just discovered that one can inject the brain of a rat with the liquid of an educated rat's memory, so that the rat which did not learn anything knows what the other had learned. We can transmit information by injection of brain memory matter, thus our children have almost no work to do. They regularly undergo injections of brain matter taken from subjects possessing the information necessary for instruction. Therefore, children are preoccupied with only interesting things, programmed by themselves, such as building the world in theory, fulfilling themselves in sports and the arts."

"You never have wars among the provinces of your world?"

"Never! The sports competitions are sufficiently developed to eliminate the war instinct. Besides, psychologically the fact that young people are able to risk their lives in games where there are systematically many deaths during each event, suppresses the war instinct by enabling those who feel it too intensely to satiate it, at the peril of their own life, and without involving those who do not want to be involved along such perilous paths. If on earth there were sports and games even more dangerous, but organised, it would greatly lessen the possibilities of creating international conflicts."

"Are the seven provinces of your world similar?"

"No, here, as on earth, there are different races and cultures. Our provinces were created and based on those races and cultures, while respecting the freedom and independence of each one."

"Would it be possible for a man to visit your planet?"

"Yes, but you would be obliged to wear a space suit, adjusted for your breathing. You could live without such a suit in a special residence where we have reproduced the earth's atmosphere, and in fact where many earthmen live, like Moses, Elijah, Jesus Christ, and many other living testimonies of our creation whom we will be able to bring back to earth when the time comes to support your statements."

"Why not bring them back at once?"

"Because in your incredulous world, if Jesus Christ returned he would be placed in a psychiatric institution. Imagine a man landing among you, saying he is the 'Christ' He would certainly be mocked at and quickly committed. If we intervene, by realising scientific wonders to show he really is the 'Christ', that would bring back the religion based on 'God', and give support to the supernatural or the mystical, which we do not want either."

Then the small man saluted me for the last time, after telling me that he would return only when what he asked of me is accomplished, and he climbed into his machine, which took off and disappeared as it had on the other mornings.

Raelian Movement

What a story! What a revelation! Upon returning home, while classifying and recopying the notes I had taken, I realised the immensity of the mission that had been entrusted to me, and felt I had little chance of carrying it out. But since it is not necessary to hope in order to undertake, I decided to do exactly what was asked of me, even though I might be taken for a visionary. After all, if being a visionary means having seen the light, then I am quite willing to be considered a visionary. It is better to be called a visionary and know the truth, than to be called a clear minded person and not know the truth.

I wish to emphasise to sceptics of all kinds that I never drink alcohol and that I sleep very well at night. One can neither dream for six consecutive days, nor invent all this.

To you who refuse to believe me, I say: Watch the sky and you will see more and more frequent apparitions that neither our scientists nor our military men will be able to explain, except by foolish babblings to save the faces which they believe they would lose if the truth did not originate from someone in their closed circle. How could a scientist possibly not know! Just as those who condemned Copernicus because he dared to say that the earth was not the centre of the Universe, could never admit that someone other than themselves could reveal all that.

But all you who have seen, or will see, unidentified flying objects, that some will qualify as mirages, or weather balloons, or even hallucinations; all of you who dare not talk about it for fear of being mocked, it is only by grouping yourselves together and by speaking to those who believe that you will be able to speak freely.

All these revelations brought me such a sense of well-being and such an inner peacefulness, in this world where we do not know what to believe, where we cannot believe in a 'white bearded God' or in a 'hoofed devil', and where the official scientists are unable to give precise explanations of our origins and our goals.

In the light of these amazing revelations, everything becomes so clear and seems too simple. Knowing that there exists somewhere in the Universe, a planet full of people who created us similar to them, who love us all the while fearing that those they had created might surpass them, is it not profoundly moving! Especially if we understand that soon it will be our priviledge to participate in the evolution of this humanity of which we are a part, by ourselves creating life on other worlds.

Now that you have read this book I have written,

trying to reproduce as clearly as possible all that was said to me, you will perhaps think that I have a great imagination and that these writings were simply to amuse you, I shall be profoundly disappointed. Perhaps these revelations will give you confidence in the future and allow you to understand the mystery of the creation and the destinies of man, thus replying to the many questions that one poses during the night, since childhood, asking why we exist and what is our purpose on this earth. If this occurs I shall be very happy indeed.

Finally, if you understand that all I have said in this book is the profound truth and wish, as I wish, to see these men come officially very soon to give us their heritage, then participate in the realisation of all that has been asked of me. Only then will the purpose of this book be fulfilled. If so, then write to me and we will welcome you into the Raelian Movement, we will build the residence they wish and, when we are numerous enough all over the world, and waiting for them with the respect and love that is justly demanded by those who created us, then they will come and we will be the beneficiaries of their immense knowledge.

All you who believe in God or in Jesus Christ, you are right in believing. Even if you thought all was not exactly as they would have you believe, there was a foundation of truth. You are right in believing in the foundation of the scriptures, but wrong to maintain the Church. If now you continue to distribute your money to provide the cardinals with the finest vestments, to authorise the existence of the military with their atomic menace, all at your expense, then it means that you wish to stay primitive and are not interested in the golden age to which you are entitled. If, however, you wish to participate passively or actively in the creation and development of the Movement for the Elohim, Creators of Humanity, take your pen and write to me. We will very soon be numerous enough to undertake the choice of a piece of ground whereon will be built the residence. If you still have doubts, read the newspapers and look at the sky where you will see that the appearances of the mysterious machines will be more and more numerous and you will gain the courage to send your letter.

Claude RAEL

INTERNATIONAL RAELIAN MOVEMENT
C.P. 225
CH-1211 GENEVA 8
SWITZERLAND

THE EXTRA-TERRESTRIALS TOOK ME TO THEIR PLANET

THE EXTRA-TERRESTRIALS TOOK ME TO THEIR PLANET

Introduction

I simply wanted to relate what my life was like before my fantastic encounter of December 13, 1973, to answer the many people who have asked me what I did before and if extraordinary events had happened to me during my childhood which enabled me to foresee such a destiny. I was, myself, surprised in searching my memories, for whereas I thought that nothing extraordinary had occurred at the beginning of my life, in fact, certain scenes came to the surface, scenes which, when put together, formed a whole, and showed that my life had indeed been guided in order for me to be what I was and in order to find myself at the place where I found myself on December 13, 1973.

When I had practically finished writing all these, the second encounter took place. I then summed these up as much as possible to give much more room to the second message and to the narration of the second contact which is still more fantastic than the first.

CHAPTER I
MY LIFE TILL THE FIRST ENCOUNTER

Two Years Already

My Childhood, U.F.O. Over Ambert

The Pope of The Druids

Poetry

The Encounter

The Lectures

Two Years Already

Two years! It's been almost two years now since I've been trying to radiate this truth too huge for me. Time goes by and I have the impression of getting nowhere. And yet there is a solid core of people forming around me little by little who understood that the First Message was really saying the Truth. Seven hundred, they are seven hundred at present as I write these lines in neat and I understand to what extent they are both few and many at the same time. Few when we think of the four billion men who populate the earth, and many when we think of the small number of people who after two years had decided to follow the one who, two thousand years ago, had the equally heavy burden of being initiated and of initiating the primitives of his time. These seven hundred, who are they? Are they, as it would without doubt please the scoffers, average "simpletons" who could be made to swallow anything? Well no! Some of them are even graduates, or doctors in philosophy, psychology, theology, sociology, medicine, physics, chemistry, etc. But my admiration goes maybe as much to those who have no degree, because even without having through their studies acquired the knowledge enabling them to understand that living matter and men like us can be scientifically created, they were able to feel it intuitively, as men capable of mastering matter and putting themselves in harmony with the universe which they are part of.

However, I must say above all that I am quite optimistic and I believe that I have, as I write, led the mission which has been entrusted to me on the right path for whatever happens to me, the MADECH(2) is on its way and nothing will be able to stop it.

In two years I have given nearly forty lectures, and some questions have come up regularly, and I suppose that some passages of the message need to be clarified, which is what I will try to accomplish in this work. First of all what sort of life did I lead before the encounter of December 13, 1973? I must confess that it has been just a short time since I have looked back on myself to see exactly how my life has been guided, to be available and ready to enter into action on the spiritual, psychic and neural levels at this time. Some events of my childhood did not appear to have any real significance taken separately but did when taken together. Now everything seems very clear and I remember with emotion these moments which I thought then were not of great interest. It is not my intention to tell the story of my life considering that each event of it is exceptional but it appears that many people wanted to know more about what had happened to me "before". Instead of letting wagging tongues say anything I prefer to tell it all myself . . . .

(2) In 1975, with the authorization of the Elohim, the movement was changed to the Raelian Movement.

My Childhood, U.F.O.Over Ambert

Born of an unknown father, I cannot say that I had an average childhood. I was what they call a natural child (as if the others were artificial children . . .), an accident as it were, at least for this little town of Ambert, world capital of the rosary (sic) and on top of that, oh sacrilege, the unknown father (not so unknown as . . .) was, it seems, a Jewish refugee! My birth was concealed as much as possible, not in a cave, but in a clinic at Vichy. I was born on September 30th, 1946 at about two o'clock in the morning and it was a very difficult birth. But what is important is that I was conceived on December 25th, 1945. The conception, the moment at which the being really begins to exist and develop in the womb of its mother, is the date of true birth of each individual. December 25th has been a very important date for almost two thousand years now. For those who believe in coincidence, then my life began with a coincidence . . . .

Then we returned to Ambert near to where her father lived, where my poor mother tried for a long time to pretend that I was "the son of a friend whom she was taking care of for a while". If he held it against her after learning the truth, he was the nicest of grandfathers towards me during the short time that I knew him. Unfortunately, he died when I was still a very little child, and I was told later about the amused look that he had when, seeing him trim his fruit trees, I took his scissors to cut . . . his lettuce!

I was raised by my grandmother and my aunt who were, and are, still living together. They taught me how to read and helped me take my first steps which I remember very clearly and certainly that is the earliest thing of my life that I remember.

It is only very recently that my grandmother told me about the strange machine that she saw over Ambert in 1947 flying noiselessly and very fast near her house. She never dared to tell anyone about it for fear of being accused of having hallucinations. It was only after reading my book that she decided to tell me about it, at the time she decided to join MADECH. Her joining was in fact one of the most important encouragements that I have received.

The Pope of The Druids

In Ambert there was an old man of whom the small children were afraid and whom the grown-ups made fun of. They nicknamed him Jesus Christ because he had very long hair, rolled up in a bun, and a magnificent beard. He always wore a long cape that came down to his ankles and lived a hundred meters (328 ft)* from the house where my mother had found a small apartment. He never worked and nobody knew what he lived on, in the tiny house located just in front of the municipal grammer-school. As they grew up the children lost their fear

*added in translation

of him, and like their parents, began to mock him, following him, laughing and making faces. Personally, I did not like to play with the others, preferring to contemplate insects and to look at books. I often passed that man on the street and was surprised by his face which emitted a great kindness, and by the mischievous smile that he had when he looked at me. I didn't know why, but he did not frighten me, I didn't find anything funny about him, and I didn't understand why the other children laughed at him.

One afternoon, I followed him, curious to know where he was going, and I saw him enter his small house, leaving the door open to a small very dark kitchen. I approached and saw him, sitting on a stool, and, as if he were expecting me, with a teasing smile. He motioned for me to come nearer. I entered the house and went towards him. He laid his hand on my head and I felt a strange sensation. At the same time he looked towards the sky and pronounced words which I did not understand. After a few minutes, he let me go, without saying a word and with the same mysterious smile.

All this puzzled me at the time but I very quickly forgot about it. It was only in the summer of 1974, while reading a book that my mother had lent me which mentioned the Auvergne mysteries, that I learned that father Dissard, the old man in question, was the last "Dissard", that is to say the last "Pope" of Druids still alive, and who died a few years ago. Then I recollected the scene of my childhood and I thought again about the mysterious smile of the old man each time I passed him on the street, that is to say everyday, as we were neighbours or almost neighbours. I know now exactly to whom he spoke, looking towards the sky pronouncing these mysterious phrases, just as I know exactly what the luminous and silent machine was that my grandmother had seen. Another thing comes to my mind: from the time of what happened at father Dissard's house onwards, I fell asleep each night counting up to nine a number of times, the number that has frequently come up throughout my life, like a code which had been assigned to me. I have never been able to explain this sudden habit, which happened unexpectedly several years after I had learned to count much further than nine and therefore it was not a question of rote learning. I was seven years old when this incident took place.

Poetry

What really mattered to me at that time was animals, which I loved sketching all day long when I wasn't organizing snail races . . . . Attracted by animal life, I used to dream of becoming an explorer so that I could be closer to the mysterious fauna of the virgin forests.

But at the age of nine (nine again) everything changed. First, I discovered what was to become a real passion for me: the speed on wheels with or without a motor, speed and especially balance, the sense of trajectories and the struggle against myself,

against my own reflexes, basically, the perfect domination of the body by the mind.

At first, it was the wild runs on a small almost brakeless bicycle and I wonder how come I didn't fall once. To complicate it all, I positioned myself on top of a hill and waited until a very fast car went past. Then I would throw myself into dizzy pursuit, catching and overtaking the car to the driver's great surprise and having arrived at the end of the descent, I would make half a turn and go back to wait at the high place for another car . . . .

A few months later, by chance I was at the passing of the Tour de France automobile race and it was "love at first sight"; to know one could then enjoy speed without having to pedal back up the hill. And one could do it as a profession. My decision was made, the way one decides at nine years old: I would become a racing car driver!.

From that day on, my life was centered only around automobile competitions, nothing else interested me and I did not see any use in learning all the things they told me at school since I was going to be a racing car driver! The comic strips were replaced by very serious automobile magazines and I started impatiently to count the number of years separating me from the age when I could have a driver's license.

It was also at nine years old that I was first sent to boarding school. My mother, desperate because I didn't want to do anything at school, and because I repeated constantly that I didn't need this to become a racing car driver, had decided to put me into the

Notre-Dame-De-France private school, in Puy-en-Velay. She hoped that this way, without racing car magazines, I would put myself to work, and in a way she wasn't far wrong. But I have unpleasant memories of that first boarding school, probably because I was too young when I was enrolled. I remember many nights spent crying in that huge dormitory where, what I believe I missed the most, was the possibility of being alone to meditate. This, as well as my emotional and affective needs, which made me cry all night long, increased my already very great sensitivity. I then discovered poetry.

In any case, I had always been more attracted by French than by mathematics, but always as an interested but passive reader. Then came the desire, the need, to write, in verse if possible. Even if I remained uninterested in mathematics, I was now average in that subject as in all the others, except in French and specially in composition where I was regularly first so long as the subject pleased me. I wrote a whole collection of poems and won first prize in a poetry contest.

The most surprising thing was that even though I had not been baptized I was in a private boarding school run by Catholic brothers with all that it implies (prayer before eating, before going to bed, when we got up, before studying, etc. . . .) including daily mass with communion . . . . After six months of daily communion, the brothers were horrified when they finally discovered that I had not been baptized. I thought it was funny, in fact it was the only part of their mass which I liked, this free tasting of crumbs of bread . . . .

It was also at nine years old that I reached the age of puberty. I enjoyed it very much and it was even a consolation for my incomplete solitude, discovering unknown and secret pleasures, which no other nine year old children in the dormitory seemed to know about yet.

Finally, it was at the age of nine that I fell in love for the first time, the type of love children of that age fall in. Since my schoolwork was good, my mother had accepted not to send me back to the boarding school and I ended up in the eighth grade at the municipal grammer school of Ambert. There she was, almost nine years old, her name was Brigitte, and I was shy and blushing, and so ridiculous. It took but a look during a medical visit, a gesture of modesty to hide from my eyes a bust where there was obviously nothing to see, to release in me feelings of tenderness and a great desire to protect that apparently so fragile being.

The following year, I found myself at the same school, in the seventh grade, in the company of my first love whom I didn't even dare talk to. I had managed to sit one desk in front of her at the beginning of the school year so I could turn my head from time to time and admire her beloved face. I was only ten and was always thinking about her.

The fact that I was close to her in class stimulated me and so I started to work sufficiently so that I wouldn't repeat a year. I then went to the sixth grade still without the slightest liking for my studies but unfortunately we kept changing classes and now had different teachers instead of one form-master. Consequently, I was always away from her and I almost stopped working. So much so that the next year I found myself back in a boarding school in a small village situated at about thirty kilometers (about 19 miles*) from Ambert: Cunlhat.

It was even worse there than at Puy-en-Valey. We were one on top of the other in a small dormitory which was almost never heated, and what's more, there was virtually no discipline and the biggest, namely, the strongest kids, enforced their law. I think that's where I developed such a hatred for violence. One day, fed up with being bullied by the strongest boys and with no disciplinary measures taken against them, I took to the road on foot, determined to make the thirty kilometers to mother's house. Nobody had noticed my departure and when the school principal finally reached me with his car, I had already walked nearly ten kilometers (about 6 miles*).

To my great joy, I was kicked out in the middle of the school year and brought back to the brothers at Ambert as a day student. Oh what joy, I could come across Brigitte every day in the street, still as beautiful as ever, and on whom twelve springs had made her bust deliciously budding.

Being less and less interested in studies, I started to

*added in translation

taste the joys of playing truant, especially as I didn't particularly appreciate finding myself 'at the priests', who had advised my mother to have me baptized . . . . Fortunately, she preferred to wait until I was old enough to understand so she could ask my opinion.

What I would have liked at the time, was to become a mechanic because I had learned that it was useful for a racing driver. My mother, who would have liked me to become an engineer, wanted me at all costs to continue with my studies and did not allow me to become a garage apprentice. That new vexation again gave me the desire to write poems and I started taking walks in the country with a notebook in my hand instead of going to classes.

At fourteen, I was back in boarding school, this time in Mont-Dore, in the grammar-school where they accept children not wanted by all the other schools in the region. I was amongst a group of dunces and some fairly interesting "hard-cases". It was one of the hard headed ones, one of the boarding school "leaders" who was responsible for the orientation of the next ten years of my life. His name was Jacques and he played the electric guitar, which quite impressed me. As soon as the Christmas holidays came, I got my grandmother to buy me a magnificent guitar so that Jacques could teach me a few chords. Then I started putting my poems to music and noticed that apparently it was very pleasing to those who were listening. As soon as the summer vacation came I started to enter some radio contests which I almost always won.

It was also during the summer vacation that I learned about physical love for the first time, with a bar maid who was enchanted by my songs. She was twenty years old and didn't teach me much other than the powers my guitar had over women.

The following year I was fifteen and had more desire than ever to live my life. One day, I grabbed my guitar and a small suitcase, I said goodbye to the boarding school with its uninteresting studies and hitch-hiked my way to Paris.

I had two thousand old francs in my pocket and a heart full of hope. At last, I was going to earn my living by myself and be able to save to pass my driver's license at the age of eighteen in order to become a racing driver.

By a stroke of luck, I was picked up by a man driving a car which hid powerful acceleration under the body of a discreet travelling coach, and when he told me his name and that he was a racing driver, I was able to tell him which car he had driven and the classification he had obtained. He was flattered and stunned to meet a young boy remembering all his records. He told me that he had once been a clown and that he now owned a garage in the South West. When we arrived in Paris he invited me out to dinner and even offered me a room in the hotel where he was staying. There, we chatted a bit with two young women in the lounge who were dance hostesses in a bar and had finished their day's work; I sang some songs and then we went to bed each with one of the charming companions. There, I was really initiated to physical love making.

The next morning I left discreetly because I wanted to find a room and some cabarets which would be interested in my songs. I found neither and I spent my second night in Paris in the metro with the bums. I had no more money left and the next morning I was starving. I spent the whole day just hanging around losing hope of ever sorting anything out. But during the evening, I saw a man playing the accordion on a cafe terrace, and the customers were throwing him coins. I decided to try the same thing and right from the start it worked very well. I was saved.

I lived like that for three years, often sleeping anywhere and eating a sandwich from time to time. I was making a lot of progress and one day I was hired by a small cabaret on the left bank. I was earning ten francs per night but needed fifteen francs for the taxi back to Montmartre hill where I lived in a small room .... But my name was printed on the poster (in small print ...)! And already I was imagining my name in big letters on the poster seeing the success I had every night. One day, I met the comedian Jean-Pierre Darras who advised me to take an acting course to improve my stage presence, and since I didn't have the means, he arranged it himself so that I could attend the T.N.P.* course without any charge. For three months I attended the Dullin course, and then I abandoned it because I did not feel attracted at all by

*theatre in Paris

the theatre.

I used to introduce myself at the time under the pseudonym of Claude Celler, which I had chosen as a tribute to the skier and champion racing car driver, Tony Sailer, but modifying the spelling so that my initials would become C.C.

I then won many radio contests and, by singing in several cabarets, I was able to live more or less well, and most importantly save enough money to pass my driver's license at eighteen as I had always intended. But that wasn't enough to become a racing driver. First I had to make a name for myself so that I would be hired by a company, and for that, I had to have a competitive car, participate in some races independently and if possible win them. However, a racing car is very expensive. So I had to continue saving to be able to acquire such a vehicle. I continued therefore with my singing, and tried to put some money aside. Many writer-composer friends had made some recordings and seemed to be making a lot of money. So I decided to try to make a recording, having by now one hundred and fifty songs in my bag.

The first recording firm that I went to offered me a three year contract which I signed. The director of the recording firm was Lucien Morisse, director of the radio station "Europe No. 1", and who had introduced a tremendous number of famous singers. My first record was fairly successful, and the second record, thanks to a song called "Le Miel et la Canelle", was even more popular. Maybe the words might help you to remember the music as it was often heard on the radio:

Le Miel Et La Canelle

Ça sent le miel et la canelle
Ça sent la vanille et l'amour
Ça sent le miel et la canelle
Filles que j'aimerai toujours.

La première était brune et s'appelait Margot
Le soir au clair de lune nous jouions du flutiau
Moi j'ai pris la route de ses yeux
Et le chemin sans doute de ses cheveux.

La deuxième était blonde et s'appelait Marielle
Les sentiers de sa rounde encore je me rappelle
Moi j'ai pris la route de ses yeux
Et le chemin sans doute de ses cheveux.

La troisième était rousse et s'appelait Marion
Pour sa jolie frimousse et son conquin jupon
Moi j'ai pris la route de ses yeux
Et le chemin sans doute de ses cheveux.

Ne pleure pas l' ami, demain c'est le printemps
Elles sont si jolies et tu n'as pas vingt ans
Moi j'ai pris la route de ses yeux
Toi tu prendras la route de ses cheveux.

Cinnamon-Honey

It smells of cinnamon-honey
The scent of vanilla and love
It smells of cinnamon-honey
The girls whom I'll always love.

The first was brunette, Margot was her name
We played the pipes as the moon lit the night
I took the road to her eyes
And followed the way to her hair.

The second was blond, Marielle was her name
The verges of her curves, I remember so well
I took the road to her eyes
And followed the way to her hair.

The third had red hair, Marion was she called
For her lovely buzz and her cute little skirt
I took the road to her eyes
And followed the way to her hair.

Don't cry my friend, for tomorrow will be spring
They are so pretty and you're not twenty yet
I took the road to her eyes
And you'll try the path to her hair.

I was then doing numerous performances and participated in many road shows. Everything was going well and I even had the pleasure of being selected to participate in the Golden Rose of French

Songs in Antibes.

But those who guided me didn't really want me to become too famous an artist. That stage of my life was for developing my sensitivity and getting me used to expressing myself in public, but no more than that.

Even though every morning they announced over the radio that I was among the selected competitors of the Golden Rose which was to take place a week later, one day Lucien Morisse came to me and explained that he was forced to withdraw me from the contest, and that I would understand why later but that he couldn't tell me more at that moment. In the end I did not participate in the Golden Rose.

I continued therefore to live poorly from the songs and I realized that I would never win enough to buy myself the car which would send me to the race track. So, when I was offered the opportunity to become a representative for the record firm where I recorded, I accepted immediately, convinced that I would be able to save enough money that way in a few months.

I found myself back in Bordeaux, where I was in charge of about fifteen departments for which I was responsible as their commercial agent. I stayed there one year and left as soon as I had enough to buy myself (finally . . . .) a competitive vehicle.

Unfortunately, I only had just enough time to run in that car before it was destroyed in an accident by a friend . . . But I had written new songs during the past year in the South West and a wealthy friend urged me to make another record which he would finance himself.

I spent another year living on my poetry and then, as if to make me definitely change my lifestyle, I had a very serious car accident. During a very tiring tour I fell asleep at the wheel and hit a wall head on at about one hundred kilometers (63 miles)* per hour. At least ten people had already died at the same spot. I came out of it with fractures, but alive. Immobilized for more than three months, my savings disappeared and I still wasn't racing! I had dreamed of beginning at the age of eighteen, at twenty-two I had still never entered a race....

Having gone so many times to the circuits as a spectator, I had noticed young people's infatuation for that sport and the number of boys wishing to become racing drivers without knowing how to proceed. I didn't know much more than they did but I said to myself that the best way that I could find to approach that environment was to find a profession exploiting the infatuation of young people for that specialty. I knew how to write, the solution was found: I could become a reporter for a sports car magazine. I made some contacts with specialized magazines, but in vain because many other young people had the same idea.

Then I noticed a small ad in the car section of "L'Equipe". They were looking for photographer-reporters even without experience. I wrote and they answered that my application was being considered,

*added in translation

and that I had to give one hundred and fifty francs for the expenses of file research. In exchange, I would receive a film in order to make a test report on the subject of my choice. I sent the money, received the film and carried out the report, obviously on a car race, which I immediately sent back to the indicated address.

Very soon I received a letter asking me to telephone Dijon, where the head office of the enterprise which had done the small ad was. Afterwards I met the head of that "publishing" company, a man of about thirty years old who claimed that he had "made a fortune" in photography in the United States, and who seemed to be very interested in my ideas concerning the creation of a sports car magazine intended for young people wishing to become racing car drivers. He finally offered to hire me as an editor-in-chief of a newspaper which was to come out a few months later. He showed me the factory that he was going to buy to install his printing office, he introduced me to the printer of Dijon whom he had hired as director, and showed me the house my wife and I would live in, at about two steps from my office. I answered that it was convenient for me on the condition that I could participate in and keep in contact with the racing world. He then told me that if I preferred, he was also looking for someone able to manage a competition department, since he intended to launch the new newspaper by running racing cars painted in his own colors. That would permit me to be exactly where the action was and I accepted to become the director of the competition service for that company.

A week later, I moved with my wife from Paris to Dijon. I had been married for about three months and my wife was already expecting a child. I had met Marie-Paul in the month of June and we had not left each other ever since that first day we met. We were married three months later, only because her family was shocked to learn that we didn't have any intentions of getting married religously. It was a family full of principles, and where there were, at the beginning, prayers before meals . . . .

My stay in Dijon only lasted two months, without any salary, and it transpired that the rich American who wanted to create a newspaper had in fact just come out of prison without a penny!!! He had swindled a sum of money ranging from between one hundred and fifty to three hundred francs from more than five hundred young persons dreaming like me of becoming racing car drivers or photographer-reporters. I had worked two months for nothing and I found myself with my ideas and penniless.

This time, I decided to make a start all alone in the big world of publishing. I moved to Clermont-Ferrand, close to my mother so she could know the joys of soon being a grandmother, and I created a publishing house for me to publish the magazine "in my own way". That magazine was soon born thanks to a printer who also loved sports cars and who agreed to take the risk of giving me credit, although I didn't have any guarantee to give him.

The journal started quickly and very fast became one of the best in that field. The best part was that I reserved for myself the most interesting task: test driving new models on the magnificent circuit of Mas-du-Clos, in Creuse, and on the road. I could then be introduced to that not easily accessible environment of racing and have cars lent to me for racing. At last my dream was becoming a reality, and what is more I noticed that I was very gifted, winning many victories from the start with cars that were unfamiliar to me.

I lived three marvellous years, continuously progressing in driving and technique and living one hundred percent in the field that I loved: that of sports cars. I must say that I felt a real pleasure to always push back my limitations and to control my reflexes and my reactions better and better. Neither the sound of the motor, nor the odor of the burned fuel interested me and I must admit that I loved to dream about a new rule obliging the racing car manufacturers to make the cars odorless and noiseless, in order to enjoy only the sensations of driving at its purest level.

And all this was upset on the 13th of December, 1973 . . . .

The Encounter

That is roughly what had happened before the extraordinary day of December the 13th, 1973, where in a crater of an Auvergne volcano, the Puy-de-La-Sola, I met for the first time that extra-terrestrial man, or more precisely the Eloha (in plural, Elohim) whom I would meet at the same place for six consecutive days and who, each time for about one hour, dictated to me the first message and his fantastic revelations. In fact, I was wrong in calling the place Puy-de-la-Vache, which is the name of the volcano situated next to Puy-de-la-Sola.*

The first days, I must confess that I wondered if I should dare to tell anyone about it. First of all, I made a neat copy of the notes I had taken as best as I could though much too quickly, while my interlocutor spoke. When all this was finished, I sent the original manuscript to a publisher whom I judged serious, since to my knowledge he did not publish esoteric works or science fiction, and I obviously did not want this message of capital importance to humanity to be found drowned among mysterious adventure collections or dark books which cultivate people's interest in these parallel sciences.

Marcel Jullian, who directed that publishing house, asked me to come to Paris and told me that it was sensational but that I absolutely had to tell my life story before talking about the message and that there

*see First Message

might be "a few changes to be made". This was absolutely out of the question. I didn't want to spend a hundred pages talking about my life and then present the message that I had received, as if my personality was as important as that which I had been requested to reveal. I wanted the message published, but only the message, even if it wasn't a thick book and therefore not very interesting for a publisher. So I asked Mr. Jullian to return my manuscript. He answered that he didn't have it because a reader had borrowed it, but that as soon as it was returned, he would mail to me.

I was hardly back at Clermont-Ferrand, when I received a telegram asking me to come to Paris to attend a television broadcasting of Jacques Chancel, the Great Chess-Master. As the director of a collection in the publishing house where I had sent my manuscript, he had read it and understood that it was absolutely fantastic whether or not one believed it. I participated therefore in the show and the thousands of letters which I received showed me that, although some people made fun of me, many had taken it very seriously and wanted to help. But the days went by and I still had not received my manuscript. I sent a registered letter to the publisher who answered that the manuscript would be sent to me but that they had not yet found it. After ten days, I went back to Paris to do "something" because nobody would answer me any more when I telephoned to ask if they had received it. The famous designer Courrèges, who had contacted me after the television show because he was interested, offered to come with me to the publisher in order to find out what exactly had become of the manuscript. Mr. Jullian told us that the reader who had taken the message had gone on vacation with it and that they did not know where to contact him . . . stranger and stranger . . . . It was finally Mr. Courrèges who got the manuscript back and returned it to me personally. I still wonder if it was really lost or just put away to prevent it from being published. And if that publishing house really misplaced the manuscript so easily, then I would discourage any authors from sending them their originals . . . .

Alarmed by the mishap and by the growing pile of letters from people interested in buying the book containing the message as soon as it was published, Marie-Paul offered to leave her nursing job to help me with the publishing and the distribution of that exceptional document. I accepted, because I was sure that in this way, I would be permanently in control of its use.

I immediately ceased working for the sports magazine, which was incompatible with the seriousness of the mission given to me, and in the autumn of 1974, the book finally came off the printing press.

The nervous shock caused by the unforseeable upset of my existence had subsequently given me stomach-aches, almost bringing on an ulcer, a serious gastritis which made me suffer all winter. No medication was effective, and it was only after deciding to take it easy by doing some meditation and breathing exercises that the pains vanished as if by magic.

In June, I participated in a television show hosted by Philippe Bouvard: "Saturday evening", and, sarcastic as usual, he disguised his co-host as a "Martian" with pink antennas and a green suit and asked me if he resembled the person I had met .... But the public at large, interested by the little I had been able to say, wrote to Philippe Bouvard reproaching him for his lack of seriousness. And confronted by thousands of letters he received, he decided to get me back to do another show where I would be able to say a little more ....

Convinced that in no way would I be allowed to say enough, I decided to rent the Pleyel Hall for a date just after the television show, and to announce to the interested viewers that I was giving a lecture at that place in a few days time. I rented a hall of one hundred and fifty seats with an option of five hundred seats without knowing how many people would wish to bother to come and listen to me: There were over three thousand people! Quite understandably we had to evacuate the hall for security reasons and let in only the pre-arranged number required to fill the room, and advise the others that I would give another lecture a few days later in a large hall of two thousand seats. Evidently, some people were not happy to leave, having travelled a few hundred kilometers.

Everything finally went well and I was able to ascertain that, aside from the scoffers whose questions, by virtue of their own superficiality, I was able to show up as ridiculous anyway, a great number of people were ready to help and support me. Even though I had dreadful "stage-fright", much more than I had ever had when singing, everything went without problem, while the answers to the most difficult questions seemed to come by themselves to my lips. I really felt some help coming from above, just as they had promised me. I had the impression of listening to myself answering things that I could not have found out by myself. The second lecture took place a few days later. I was very afraid that those who had not been able to attend the first time would not come back and I would therefore find myself with an expensive hall nearly empty. Especially as there had not been any publicity about it since the television program, except for the three lines in "France-Soir", the only newspaper which agreed to announce my second lecture. Again there were more than two thousand people and the hall was full! It was a triumph. This time I did not have any doubts about the success of my mission.

The Lectures

Thus, since the month of September, I saw, during some forty lectures, the questions that came up most frequently, the number of MADECH members constantly rising and the regional offices being formed in all the big towns of France, around the most dynamic members. I also saw some reporters doing a really good job, which consisted of informing their public by writing or by saying exactly what they had seen or read about, while other reporters, as those from *Le Point* newspaper, wrote lies. Even after registered letters reminding them that, according to the right of response, they had to rectify the slandering article, they did not rectify the writing exactly; others, as those at *La Montagne* newspaper, had simply refused to inform the readers that I was giving a lecture at Clermont-Ferrand, and took advantage of the fact that they were the only daily newspaper in the region. The news director of this newspaper had met me and told me that they would never mention me or my activities in his newspaper. All this because they did not like the fact that when I appeared for the first time on television, I had not informed them first before talking to the ORTF (French Broadcasting)* . . . . A gloomy story and a nice example of the freedom of speech. They even refused to run a paid advertisement announcing that lecture. While in the same newspaper, there were full page ads for pornographic films . . . . As for *Le Point* newspaper, it had simply transformed an excursion of MADECH members to the place where the encounter occurred into a broken appointment with the Elohim . . . . And the trick is played in an attempt to ridicule an organization trying to get off the ground. It is evidently easier and less dangerous for a newspaper with extensive readership to do it against the MADECH than against the Church with its two thou-

*added in translation

sand year history of usurpation. But a day will come when those who have tried to hide or deform the truth will regret their mistakes.

CHAPTER 2
THE SECOND ENCOUNTER

The Sighting of July 31st, 1975

The Second Message

Buddhism

Neither God nor Soul

The Paradise on Earth

The Other World

Meeting The Ancient Prophets

A Foretaste of Paradise

The New Commandments

To The People of Israel

The Sighting of July 31st, 1975

It was in the month of June 1975 that I decided to resign as president of MADECH. One, because it seemed that the movement could now manage very well without me, and two, because I thought I had made a mistake in structuring that organization according to the 1901 law, which compared this movement so capital for humanity, with an association of petanque (French bowl game*) players or war veterans .... I thought it was necessary to create a movement more in accordance with the fantastic message the Elohim had transmitted to me, that is to say a movement respecting literally what had been advised by our Creators, namely geniocracy, humanitarianism, the renouncing of all deistic religious practices, etc. The law of the 1901 type association was by definition, contrary to the meaning of the message, at least in the form under which we had structured it since all members could vote. Thus the principles of geniocracy were not being respected, which require namely that only the most intelligent ones take part in making decisions. I therefore had to correct this fundamental mistake, not by dissolving the MADECH, but rather by transforming it into an association (which the regulation of the 1901 law could not obstruct) until more efficient modifications regarding its structure could be implemented. The

*added in translation

MADECH would help the movement that I was now going to create with its most open minded members; that is to say, this undeclared association would be a congregation of MADECH guides, gathering together people wanting to open other peoples' minds to infinity and eternity by scrupulously applying what was asked in the message and becoming guides for humanity. In a society seeking in every way to close people's minds with desitic religions, soporific education, anti-thought television shows and narrow-minded political fights, I was thus going to try to initiate people who would go throughout the world, trying to open the minds of others. The MADECH was now becoming a support organization, having the first contact with those discovering the message and so retaining its importance. In a way, the MADECH was becoming a supportive movement made up of "practising members" and the congregation of guides was going to be a movement made up of "monks" guiding the practising members. I knew that among the members there were capable, strong people able to manage the MADECH and I had confirmation of this during the administration's council elections. My substitute as president, Christian, was a physicist with prospects and the rest of the council was made up of people who were all equally representative and competent.

It was also in the month of June that Francois, one of the most devoted members of MADECH and equally one of the most open minded, came to see me in Clermont-Ferrand. I told him about my desire of finding a country house in a place as secluded as possible so that I would be able to rest a little and write peacefully a book about what had happened to me before December the 13th 1973, before anyone could invent a whole load of rubbish about my past. He told me that he had a farm in an out-of-the-way place in Périgord, and if I liked the area, I could go there for a month or two and even live there for the time that I wanted since nobody lived there.

Then we left very quickly by car to visit the place, and seeing the calmness and the serenity of the region, I decided to go for two months. After fifteen days, I loved it so much that I was seriously considering settling there more definitely. Francois came to join us at the end of July and we started anticipating my moving for the day after the reunion of the 6th of August in Clermont-Ferrand. I had still not definitely decided, being afraid of failing my mission by moving away from the place of my marvelous meeting, but on July the 31st, while we were out to get some fresh air with my wife, Marie-Paul, and Francois, we saw a machine seemingly enormous but silent, passing with jerking movements almost over the house, sometimes with unimaginable speed, then instantaneously still and moving in zigzag at about five hundred meters (1,640 ft*) from us. I was very happy that other people were with me witnessing the spectacle and a sensation of undescribable happiness overcame me then. Francois told me that the hair on his head had

*added in translation

stood on end from emotion. To me, it was an obvious sign of the Elohim's consent to my moving to that region.

The next morning, I noticed that I had a strange mark on my arm, on the biceps, close to the folding of my elbow. I didn't relate it right away to what had happened the day before, but later on people told me that it could only be a mark made by the Elohim. It was a red circle of about three centimeters (1-1/5 in*) in diameter and five millimeters (about 1/5 in*) thick inside of which were three smaller circles. The mark remained for the next fifteen days, then the three middle circles transformed themselves into one, forming two concentric circles.

After another fifteen days the two circles disappeared, leaving a white spot on my arm which I still have. I emphasize the fact that I never suffered from that mark and that I didn't feel any itching during the time I had it. Some open minded scientists to whom I showed that mark hypothesised that it could have been a sample taken with the help of a perfected laser.

The meeting of the 6th of August finally took place as planned in the crater of Puy-de-La-Sola and there at the meeting a harmony and admirable fraternity prevailed. I had decided to hold the assembly of MADECH members on that date without really knowing why, but it must have been the Elohim who had guided me, because some of the members in-

*added in translation

The Symbol found on
The Tibetan Book of the Dead
or Bardo Thodol

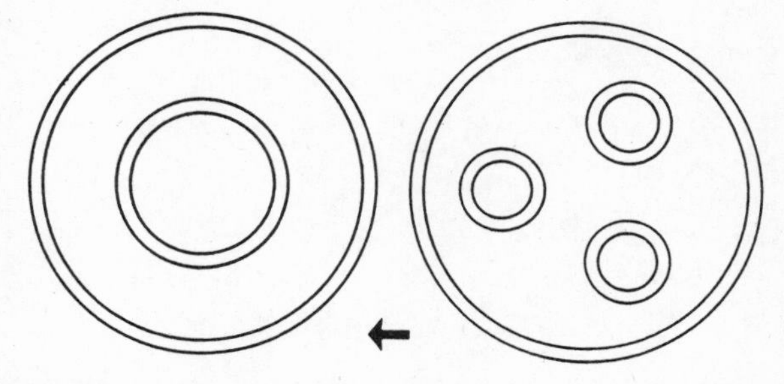

A) The sign which appeared on my arm on August 1st, 1975. The day before, a machine had flown over the house I lived in.

B) The sign A has changed and took on this ap--pearance at the end of fifteen days.

formed me on the day of the meeting that it was exactly the day of the thirtieth anniversay of the Hiroshima bomb explosion, and that it was also the day of a Christian holiday: the Transfiguration. Imbeciles will say that it was a coincidence.

After that meeting, the MADECH members helped me to move and then I settled down fully in Perigord.

The Second Message

On October 7th around eleven o'clock at night I suddenly felt the urge to go out and look at the sky. I dressed warmly because it was cold and went walking through the night. Without really being aware of it, I followed a fixed direction and I suddenly felt the need to go to a spot which Francois had shown me during the summer, a deserted place, situated between two brooks, surrounded by forests and called the Roc Plat. I got there at around midnight wondering a little what I was doing there yet, still following my intuition ever since they had told me that they could guide me telepathically. The sky was magnificent and the stars were shining everywhere, indicating that there was not a cloud around. I started watching the shooting stars when suddenly the whole countryside became illuminated and I saw a huge ball of fire, like a spark, appearing from behind the bushes. I went towards the place where the ball of fire had appeared, filled with a tremendous joy, as I was almost sure of what I would discover.

The same machine which I had seen six times during the month of December, 1973 was there, in front of me, and the same being whom I had met two years before, then came towards me with a smile full of kindness. I noticed one difference right away, he no longer had the pressurized suit which he had on the first time which seemed to make a halo around his face. I was wonderfully happy, after all that time spent trying to make the world understand that I was telling the truth, to see once more the one who was responsible for disrupting my life. I bowed in front of him and he spoke:

"Look up and follow me. We are extremely satisfied with you and everything you have done for the past two years. It is time now to pass on to the next stage since you have proved to us that we can trust you. These two years were in fact just a trial. You may have noticed that today I have no protection around the face and that my vehicle appeared to you in only one stage and that it wasn't equipped with flashing lights. All that was only meant to calm you down by appearing in a way corresponding to the image which you generally have of a space traveler. But now that you have sufficiently evolved not to be frightened, we don't use those 'approach techniques' any more."

Following him into the machine, I noticed that everything was similar inside to the one I had known at the first meeting: walls with the same metallic look as the outside, no control board or instruments, no porthole and a floor made of translucent blue substance on which were placed two armchairs made of transparent substance reminding me a little of the inflatable plastic armchairs without having an unpleasant touch. He invited me to sit down in one of the two armchairs, he settled himself in the other and asked me not to move. He then pronounced a few words in an incomprehensible language and I seemed to feel the machine rocking slightly. Then, all of a sudden, I felt a sensation of severe cold, as if my whole body was turning into a block of ice or as if thousands of crystals of ice were penetrating into all the pores of my skin, right down to the marrow of my bone. It lasted only a short time, a few seconds maybe, then I felt nothing more. Then my interlocutor rose and said:

"You may come, we have arrived."

I followed him down the small stairway. The machine was immobilized in a metallic looking circular room, about fifteen meters in diameter and ten meters in height (about 49 ft in diameter and about 33 ft high*). A door opened and my guide told me to enter and to undress completely and that I would then receive further instructions. I went into a new circular room without the slightest angle which must have been four meters (about 13 ft*) in diameter. I undressed and a voice told me to go into the room which was in front of me. At the moment a door opened and I entered into another room similar to the one I had left my clothes in but long and slightly resembling a corridor. All along that corridor there were lightings of different colours under which I passed successively. The voice then told me that I would arrive at another room by following the painted arrows on the floor, where a bath awaited me. In the next room I indeed found a sunken bathtub. The bath was luke warm, just right and discreetly perfumed. The voice advised me then to satis-

*added in translation

fy my personal needs, which I did, and then I was asked to drink the contents of a glass placed on a small shelf near the metallic wall. It was a white liquid deliciously flavored with almonds and very cold. Then a kind of pajamas which were very soft as if made of silk, were offered to me. They were white, very clinging and they awaited me on another shelf. At last another door opened and I found my guide again; he was escorted by two beings similar to him but with different features, and as welcoming as he.

I rejoined them in a huge hall where everything was astonishing. It had several levels and must have totalled one hundred meters (about 330 ft*) in diameter. It was entirely covered with an absolutely transparent dome, so transparent that at first sight it was not clear that it was a dome. Thousand of stars studded the dark sky and yet the hall was as bright as day due to a soft light of natural look. The floor was covered with furs and shaggy carpets with enchanting and astounding colors. Everywhere there were the most admirable works of art, each more beautiful than the one before, some with animated and changing colors; elsewhere there were bright red plants and others were blue, as beautiful as exotic fishes but several meters tall. Background music made of sound resembling an organ and a muscial saw with occasional choirs and with bass doing extraordinary vibrations made the flowers incline in rhythm and change colors according to the style of the score.

*added in translation

Each time someone spoke, the music became softe so that we could understand each other without diffi culty and without having to raise our voices. Finally the air was perfumed with a thousand scents whicl also changed according to the music and the place ir which we were. The room was divided into about te corners, separated at different levels, each one havin a particular character. A brooklet meandere through all this.

Then my guide, for whom both his friends seeme to have much respect and consideration, told me:

"Follow me. We shall make ourselves comfortabl since I have many things to tell you." I followed hir to a group of armchairs and sofas made of very sof black fur where all four of us sat down.

Then my guide spoke:

"I am going to give you today a second messag which will complete the one I dictated to you ir December, 1973. You don't have anything to tak notes with, but don't worry, everything that I shal say to you will remain engraved in your mind because here we have a certain technique which wil allow you to remember everything you hear. First of all, we wish to congratulate you for all you have done in the past two years but we also want to warn you that the rest of your mission may be more difficult. But never be discouraged because you will be re- warded for your efforts whatever happens now.

To begin with, we must correct a passage in the first message which you wrongly transcribed concern- ing an eventual intervention on our part to destory humanity. It must be specified that we shall not intervene. Humanity is now arriving at a turning point in its history and its future depends only on itself. If it can control its aggressiveness towards itself and its own environment, then it will reach the golden age of interplanetary civilization, universal happiness and fulfilment. On the other hand, if it gives way to violence, then it will destory itself either directly or indirectly. There is no scientific or technical problem insurmountable for human genius, so long as the human genius is in power. A being with a deficient brain can threaten worldwide peace just as a genius can bring it happiness. The sooner you set up geniocracy, the sooner you will remove the possibility of a cataclysm occurring due to people with less evolved brains. In case of a cataclysm destroying humanity, only the ones who follow you will be saved, and these will have to repopulate the devastated earth when all danger is dispersed, as has already happened in Noah's time.

Buddhism

That is what Buddhism explains, by saying that at the time of death 'the soul' of the dead must be vigilant enough to escape the numerous 'devils' otherwise it will be reincarnated, thus falling again into the cycle, whereas if it manages to escape those famous devils, it will get away from the cycle, reaching a state of bliss through awakening. In fact, it is a very good description which applies not to the individual but to humanity as a whole, which, every time it is in a position to choose, must resist those devils who can make it fall back into the cycle. Those devils represent aggressiveness against our fellow men or against nature which we live in, and the state of bliss through awakening is the golden age of civilization where science is at the service of the people, the 'paradise on earth', where the blind can see and the deaf can hear scientifically. If humanity is not sufficiently wary of these 'devils', it will fall back into the cycle of 'reincarnation' where it must start all over again from a primitive state, and while living in a hostile world with all the suffering that entails, advance progressively towards a more evolved society. That is why the swastika is found in our symbol as it does in numerous ancient writings and which signifies the cycle. It is the choice between a paradise which the peaceful use of science allows and the hell of going back to a primitive stage where man submits to nature instead of dominating it to profit from it.

In a way, this is a natural selection at the cosmic level of which species are able to leave their planet. Only those who perfectly control their aggressiveness will reach that stage. The others will self-destruct as soon as their scientific and technical expertise permits them to invent weapons powerful enough to do so. That is why we are never afraid of those who come from elsewhere to contact us. Thousands of contacts have confirmed this absolute rule in the universe: beings capable of escaping their planetary system are always peaceful. When we discover energy source powerful enough to allow us to travel out of our own solar system, it also means that we are capable of building offensive weapons of irreversible destructive forces. If at this moment we do not perfectly master our aggression, then we shall destroy ourselves and plunge back into the cycle of progression-destruction. That means that those who voyage beyond their solar system must have mastered their aggression and escaped from the cycle.

Your region of the terrestrial globe, France, is already on the right track by trying to construct Europe, and should be the first country without an army. She would thus set an example for the whole world. France's professional military men would then lay the foundations of an European army destined to maintain the peace, and eventually catalyze and become a world peace corps. Instead of being guardians of war, the military would then be guardians of peace, a title deserving much more respect. It is necessary for an important country to show the way for others to follow, and just because France abolishes compulsory military service and has her professional military men for the service of the Europe that she is trying to construct, that doesn't mean her neighboring countries will invade her.

On the contrary, this would very soon get them to follow and imitate the path taken by your country. Once the European military is unified, so can the European economy be by creating a single European currency. Then, the same process would be applied throughout the world, adding to it, as we already told you in the first message, a single world language which would become a compulsory language in every school on earth. If one country must show the way, then it should be France. It is by preaching a 'dissuasive force' that we accumulate the arms of our own destruction. With each country wishing to dissuade another (practically never knowing which), an unlucky action might then risk transforming that 'dissuasion force' into an intervention force, fatal for the whole world.

Man sees the future through what happened in the past. This is a mistake.

The past should be scoffed at, and the present should be built for the future instead of building the present on the past. You must understand that barely thirty years ago, men of advanced countries were still primitives. You are only just emerging. And there are millions of people on earth who are still primitive and incapable of seeing something in the sky without seeing it as a 'divine' manifestation . . . . You also know that deistic religions are still very strong in all the economically undeveloped countries. You must not revere people for their age, but for their intelligence, yet making sure that old people have a pleasant life. Our distant ancestors should not be respected, but instead should be shown as an example of poor limited primitives who were not able to open themselves to the universe and who have been able to hand down very few things of value from generation to generation.

Neither God nor Soul

The more primitive a people are, the more deistic the religion which flourishes there. This is made use of by visitors from other planets, for whom this is the only way of peacefully visiting those worlds which have not yet dominated their aggressiveness. If you reach that stage where you are evolved visitors of primitive worlds, you yourselves will be forced to use that system, which is in fact very amusing and consists of being considered as gods by them. In fact, this is very easy, because for primitives, anything coming from the sky must be divine . . . . Of course, you must add a bit to be respected and pleasantly received, which does no harm. We continue to do 'apparitions' on Earth to see if it still works and to see the reactions of public authorities, the governments, and the press. We amuse ourselves quite often . . . .

As we have already explained to you in the first message, there is no god, and evidently, no soul. After death, there is nothing, if science doesn't intervene. As you know, it is possible to recreate a dead organism from one of its cells, which contains this organism's physical and intellectual plans. It is proven that a being loses a few grams (1 gram = 0.035 ounce*) at the moment of its death, in fact it is merely the energy which all living beings have readily

*added in translation

available which is eliminated at that moment. And as you know, energy, like matter, has weight. You also know that we have discovered that there is organized intelligent life on the infinitely small, quite certainly as evolved as we are and comparable to what we are ourselves, and that we have proven it. Thus, we have discovered that the stars and the planets are the atoms of a gigantic being, which itself certainly contemplates other stars with curiosity. It is also highly possible that the people living on the infinitely small levels of the infinitely large person and its fellow creatures have known periods when they believed in an immaterial 'god'. You must fully understand that everything is in everything. At this moment in an atom of your arm, millions of worlds are born and others die, believing or not in a god and in a soul and while a millennium goes by, the gigantic being whose sun is an atom has only had the time to make a step. Time is in fact inversely proportional to the mass or rather to the level of the form of life. But everything in the universe is alive and is in harmony with the infinitely large and the infinitely small. The Earth is alive like all the planets and for the small mould which is humanity, it is difficult to notice it because the time-lag due to the enormous difference of mass prevents you from perceiving its palpitations. One of our red blood cells or better still, one of the atoms that makes up our body could not imagine that it forms, with its peers, a living being. Finally, whatever happens to each individual, the universal balance stays constant but if we want, at our level, to be happy, we must live in harmony with the infinitely large, the infinitely small, and with our fellowmen.

No argument trying to support the existence of any type of god or soul can hold when we consider the infinity of the universe. There cannot be a heaven in any one place, because since the universe is infinite, it cannot have a center. Besides, as I have already explained before, there cannot be any communication because the difference in mass is too great between an infinitely large entity and a universe of infinitely small entities which creates a difference in the flow of equivalent time. Finally, if we can imagine an 'immortal soul' escaping from the body after death, a very poetic image but a bit naive having been conceived in the mind of primitives, we cannot conceive of a place where it would go, for the universe is infinite. That quantity of energy which takes off at the time of death disperses in a random way, losing all identity as it blends with all the energies suspended in the surrounding air. That identity is engraved in organized matter, in the cells of the living being who has just died. That piece of matter organized itself according to the plan determined by the male and female genes forming the first cell at the time of conception.

Concerning the origin of life on earth, some might say 'your explanation does not change a thing for you cannot say what there was in the very beginning', a stupid question, which proves that the person who asks that question has no awareness of the infinity which exists in time as in space. There is neither a beginning nor an end to matter since 'nothing is lost, nothing is created, everything is transformed' as you have certainly already heard said, only its forms can change, and that following the wishes of those who have reached a scientific level permitting them to realize this.

It is the same for the infinite levels of life, which is what the second part of our emblem represents, the star of David, composed of two overlapping triangles, one in the other, which means 'what is above is like what is below'. With the swastika which signifies that everything is cyclic, in the middle of a six branched star, you have our emblem which contains all the wisdom in the world. You can also find the two assembled symbols in ancient writings like the Bardo Thodol or the Tibetan Book of the Dead and many others also.

It is evidently very difficult for a 'finite' human brain to be conscious of infinity, which explains the need to limit the universe in time and space by believing in one or several gods which one renders responsible for everything. In fact those who cannot reach a sufficient level of humanity towards the universe, accept with difficulty the notion of infinity which makes man not something exceptional, but simply a being situated at a particular time in a particular place of the infinite universe. Obviously man prefers well defined things, well framed, 'limited' as it were, to the image of his brain. Those who ask themselves if it is possible that there is life on other planets are the best example of those limited brains, and we liked very much the comparison which you made during one of your lectures of people with frogs at the bottom of their pond wondering whether there is life in other ponds.

The Paradise on Earth

You could very soon live in a genuine terrestrial paradise if only the technology which you have was actually put into service for the well-being of people instead of the service of violence, the army, or for the personal profit of a few. Science and technology can totally liberate man not only from the anxiety of hunger in the world, but can also permit man to live without the obligation to work. Machines can quite easily look after the daily chores thanks to automation. Already, in some of your most modern factories, while not so long ago several hundred people were needed to build a car, now one person is enough to simply oversee a computer which commands and carries out all the operations for building the car. In the future, even that one person can be omitted. Workers' unions will be displeased because the factory is in less and less need of personnel and more and more workers are made redundant. That is wrong. Those fantastic machines which do the work of five hundred people should enable those five hundred people to live, instead of being used to make only one person grow rich: the boss. No man should be in another's service nor work for another for a salary. The machines can easily do all the chores and undertake all the work, enabling people to dedicate themselves to the only thing for which they are made: to think, to create, to blossom. That is what happenes on our planet. Your children must no longer be raised according to those three primitive precepts: work-family-country, but on the contrary according to the following: Blossoming-freedom-universal fraternity. Work is not sacred when motivated only by need to earn just enough to live a life of hardship, it is even terribly humiliating to sell oneself, thus to sell one's life, in order to eat by doing jobs which simple machines could do. The family has always been nothing but a way for the supporters of slavery, ancient as well as modern, to force people to work harder for a fanciful familial ideal. Finally the country is only a supplementary means for creating competition between men and bringing them eagerly everyday to the sacrosanct work. Those three terms, work-family-country, have always been supported by primitive religions. But you are not primitives now! Shake off all those old dusty principles and make the most of your life on Earth which science can transform into paradise! Don't be taken in by those who speak of an eventual enemy so as to allow weapon factories to make labourers work underpaid to produce destructive arms bringing profits to big industries. Don't be taken in by those who talk to you horrified by the drop in birthrate because youth has understood it is not necessary to have many children, and that it is better to have few children in order for them to be happier. Don't be taken in by those who once again brandish under your nose how 'neighboring people will multiply and could become a threat'! They are the same ones who are partisans of the accumulation of atomic arms under the pretext of 'dissuasion' . . . . Finally, don't let yourself be taken in by those who say that the military service enables you to learn how to use a gun and that 'it can always be useful' all the while piling up nuclear missiles. They want to teach you violence, to teach you not to be afraid of killing a man like yourself under the pretext that he is wearing a different uniform, training you so it becomes a mechanical reflex after repeated practice against training targets. Don't be taken in by those who tell you that you must fight for your country! No country deserves it. Don't be influenced by those who tell you: 'What if enemies invade our country, shouldn't we defend ourselves?' Answer them that non-violence is always more efficient than violence. It is not proven that those who 'died for France' were right no matter how aggressive the aggressors were. Look at the triumph of Gandhi in India. They will tell you that you must fight for your liberty but they forget that the Gauls lost the war against the Romans and that the French are no worse off for being descendants of the conquered, having benefited from the civilization of the conquerors. Live rather in blossoming, liberation and love instead of listening to all those narrow minded and aggressive people.

The most important accessory you have to help you reach a long lasting universal peace, is television which provides genuine planetary awareness and enables us to see what goes on every day in all parts of the world and realize that the 'barbarians' who live on the other side of the frontier have the same joys, the same sorrows and the same problems as ourselves, such as observing the progress of science, the latest artistic creations, etc. Of course, you must make sure that this wonderful tool of diffusion and of communication does not fall into the hands of people using it to condition crowds by biasing information. You may really consider television to be the nervous system of humanity, which enables each one of us to be aware of the existence of others, to see them live and which keeps us from having twisted ideas about them which brings about a fear of the 'stranger'. Long ago there was the fear of neighboring tribes, then the fear of neighboring villages, of the neighboring province, and of neighboring states. There is now a fear of the neighboring race, and should this no longer exist, then there would be the fear of eventual aggressors coming from another planet . . . on the contrary, we should be open to everything that comes from outside because all fear of strangers is the proof of a primitive level of civilization. In this sense television is irreplaceable and is one of the most important stages, if not the most important stage, of all civilizations, because, in the same way as radio, it enables all those isolated cells of humanity, which men are, to be informed at all times of what others are doing, exactly as the nervous system does in the body of a living being.

The Other World

But you are probably wondering where you are. You are in a base located relatively close to the Earth. In the first message you noted that we travel seven times faster than light, that was true twenty five thousand years ago when we landed on Earth. Since then, we have made much progress and we now travel through space much faster. It takes us only a few moments to accomplish the trip which took us almot two months at that time, and we continue to progress. If you will now follow me, we will take a little trip together."

I got up and followed my three guides. We went through the chamber, and in a huge room I discovered a machine similar to the one that had brought me from Earth this far, but much bigger. It must have been about a dozen meters (about 40ft*) in diameter on the exterior and inside had four seats instead of two, placed equally face to face. We sat down like the first time and I felt again the same sensation of intense cold and this time it lasted much longer, about ten minutes. Then the machine rocked slightly and we went towards the trap-door exit. I then discovered a marvellous scenery, paradisiac, and I can't find the words to describe the enchantment of seeing those huge flowers, each more beautiful than the next, among which some unimaginable animals were walking, birds with multicolored feathers, pink

*added in translation

and blue squirrels with bear cub heads climbing in the branches of the trees bearing enormous fruits and at the same time gigantic flowers. At about thirty meters (about 98 ft*) from the machine, a small group of Elohim were waiting for us, and behind the trees, I found a set of buildings which harmonized perfectly with the vegetation and resembled bright coloured shells. The temperature was very mild, and the air was perfumed by thousands of scents of exotic flowers. We walked towards the top of a hill and the panorama which I was beginning to discover was marvellous. Innumerable brooklets were winding through the luxurious vegetation and at a distance a blue ocean was shining in the sun.

Reaching a clearing, I discovered with great astonishment a group of men similar to me, I mean men similar to those living on Earth and not Elohim. Most of them were nude or wore robes made of multicolored silks. They bowed respectfully in front of my three guides and then we all sat down in armchairs apparently carved in the rock and covered with thick furs, but which, in spite of the warmth, still stayed very fresh and comfortable. Some men came out of a small cave situated just beside us and approached, carrying trays full of fruits, grilled meats accompanied with the best sauces, and with drinks of unforgettable flavours. And always, behind each guest, were two men squatting with the courses,

*added in translation

ready to satisfy the slightest wish of those who were eating. The latter would ask them for what they desired without even paying attention to them. During the meal, a marvellous music was heard, coming from I don't know where and young women with figures as sculptural as that of the waiters, started to dance nude with incomparable grace, on the surrounding lawn.

There must have been some forty guests similar to man on Earth in addition to my three guides. There were white, yellow and black men and women who all spoke a language which I could not understand, and which resembled Hebrew.

I was sitting on the right of the Eloha whom I had met two years earlier, and to the left of the six other Elohim. Facing me was a young bearded man, very handsome and very slim, with a mysterious smile and a look full of fraternity. To his right was a man with a noble face and having a very thick and very long black beard. To his left was a more corpulent man with an Asiatic face. He had a shaven head.

Meeting The Ancient Prophets

Towards the end of the meal, my guide, started speaking to me.

"In my first message, I spoke to you about a residence existing on our planet where Earth men were kept alive thanks to the scientific secret of eternity, starting from a cell, and among whom were Jesus, Moses, Elijah, etc . . . . That residence is in fact very big, since it is a whole planet where members of the council of eternals live also. My name is Yahweh and I am the president of the council of eternals. On the planet where we are now, eight thousand four hundred Earth people are living at this moment, who, during their lives, reached a sufficient level of open mindedness on the infinite, or who permitted humanity to remove itself from its primitive level by their discoveries, their writings, their way of organizing society, their exemplary acts of fraternity, of love or of unselfishness, and besides them also live the seven hundred Elohim, members of the council of the eternals. Whatever the outcome of your mission may be, you have your place reserved here among us, in this true little 'paradise' where everything is easy thanks to science, and where we live happily and eternally. I can truly say eternally, for as on Earth, we created all life here and we are starting to understand perfectly the life of the infinitely large, that is to say of the planets and we can detect signs of old age of solar systems which will enable us to leave this one in time to create another 'paradise' elsewhere as soon as we became anxious about its survival.

The eternals who live here, whether Earth people or Elohim, can fulfil themselves as they wish, doing only what pleases them, without having to do anything except what they like, scientific research, meditation, music, painting, etc., etc . . . or nothing at all if they feel like it!

The servants whom you saw carrying the dishes a few minutes ago as well as the dancers, are only biological robots. They are created on the same basis we have used to create men on Earth, in a one hundred percent scientific way, but they are voluntarily limited and absolutely submissive to us. They are also incapable of acting without any order, and are very specialized. They don't have any aspirations of their own, and have no pleasure, except the ones that their specialization requires. They grow old and die like us but the machine which makes them, can make far more than we really need. Besides, they are incapable of suffering, of feelings and cannot reproduce themselves. Their life span is similar to ours, that is to say, with the help of a small surgical intervention, about seven hundred years. When one of them must be destroyed, because of old age, the machine which created them produces one or several others depending on our needs. They come out of the apparatus ready for function and having their normal height for they have neither growth nor childhood. They only know how to do one thing, to obey men and Elohim and are incapable of the slightest voilence. They can all be recognized by the small blue stone they wear, both men and women, between their eyes. They take care of all the dirty work and do all the work that is uninteresting. They are produced, taken care of and destroyed underground, where in fact, all the maintenance work is done by those robots and by enormous computers which regulate all the problems of nourishment, supply of raw materials, energy, etc., etc. . . . We each have an average of ten at our service and since we are a little more than nine thousand earthlings and Elohim, there are permanently ninety thousand of them, men and women.

Like the Elohim members of the council of the eternals, the eternal Earth people are not allowed to have children and agree to go through a small operation which makes them sterile, but that sterility can easily be reversed. This arrangement is aimed at avoiding undeserving people being born into this marvellous world. However, men and women eternals can unite themselves freely as they wish, and any form of jealousy is eliminated. On the other hand, men who desire to have one or more companions outside the equality relationships which exist between men and women eternals or those who don't want to live with a woman on an equal basis can have one or more absolutely submissive female 'biological robots' to whom the machine gives the exact physical appearances desired. It is the same for women who can have one or several absolutely submissive male 'biological robots'.

The machine which produces those robots gives the entity which it creates the exact physical appearance and specialization desired. There exist several types of 'ideal' men and women, regarding the shape, appearances and looks but for instance, the height, measurements, the shape of the face, etc., can be modified as one wishes. We can even submit the picture of someone whom we particularly admired or loved on Earth, and the machine will produce the exact replica.

Thus the relationships between eternals of both

sexes are much more fraternal and respectful and the unions among them are marvellously pure and high.

Because of the extraordinary level of open mindedness of those admitted here, there is never any problem between them. The majority spend almost all of their time meditating, doing scientific research, artistic compositions, inventions and creating all kinds of things. We can live in different cities of multiple architectural styles in greatly varied sites which we can modify at will. People fulfil themselves as they wish pursuing only what they like. Some find pleasure by doing scientific experiments, others by playing music, others by creating animals each time more astonishing, others by meditating or doing nothing other than making love while enjoying the numerous pleasures of this paradisiac environment, drinking from the innumerable fountains and eating juicy fruits which grow almost everywhere at any time. Here, there is no winter, we all live in a region comparable to your equator but since we can scientifically control the weather, it is always fine and not too hot. We make the rain fall during the night when and where we want.

All this and many other things which you couldn't understand all at once make this world a real paradise. Here, every one is free and can be so without danger, for they all deserve that liberty.

All things that bring pleasure are positive, as long as that pleasure is not harmful in anyway to anyone. That is why all sensual pleasures are positive, for sensuality is always an opening to the outside world and all opening is good. On Earth, you are only just emerging from all those primitive taboos which consider wrong anything to do with sex or nudity whereas there is nothing purer. Nothing is more disappointing for your Creators than to hear people say that nudity is something bad, nudity, the image of what we made! As you can see, everyone here is naked, and those wearing clothes do so because these clothes are works of art given to them by other eternals who made them with their own hands, or for elegance or decoration.

When people from Earth are admitted to the world of the eternals, at first they go through a course of chemical education, so that nothing surprises them and they understand perfectly where they are and why."

My guide, Yahweh, stopped for a moment and then continued.

"You are now sitting right in front of the man who two thousand years ago was given the responsibility of creating a movement destined to spread more broadly the message we had left to the people of Israel, the diffusion which would enable you to be understood now. That man is Jesus whom we were able to recreate from a cell which we had preserved before his crucifixion."

The handsome bearded young man sitting right in front of me gave me a smile full of fraternity.

"To his right is Moses, to his left Elijah, to the left of Jesus is sitting the one known on Earth under the name of Buddha. A little further on you can see

Muhammad in whose writings I am called Allah because out of respect they did not dare call me by name. The forty men and women present at this meal are all representatives of the religions created after our contacts on Earth."

And they all looked at me with very fraternal and amused faces most probably remembering their own surprise when arriving in this world. My guide continued:

"Now I will show you some of our installations."

He got up and I followed him. He invited me to wear a very wide belt with a huge buckle. He and his two friends had buckled on the same kind of ornament. Immediately I felt myself being lifted up from the ground and carried, at about twenty meters (about 66 ft*) above the grass, nearly level with the top of the trees, at a very great speed, perhaps one hundred kilometers (62.5 miles*) an hour, maybe more, in a particular direction. My three companions were with me. Yahweh in front and the two friends behind. A curious thing (among others . . .) was that I did not feel the wind whipping against my face at all.

We landed in a small clearing, quite close to the entrance of a small cave. We were in fact still being carried by our belts but only at one meter from the ground and much slower. We went through galleries with metal walls and arrived in a spacious hall in the center of which was an enormous machine sur-

*added in translation

rounded by about ten robots recognizable by their forehead ornament. There we landed on the ground again and took our belts off. Yahweh then said:

"Here is the machine which produces the biological robots. We are going to create one of them for you."

He made a sign to one of the robots situated near the machine, and the robot then touched certain parts of the machine. Then he made a sign to me to come close to a window about two meters (about 6.6 ft*) long and one meter (about 3.3 ft*) wide. In a blue tinged liquid, I then saw the form of a human skeleton vaguely taking shape. Then the form appeared clearer and clearer, to finally become a real skeleton. Then the nerves took shape and formed over the bones, then the muscles and finally the skin and the hair. A splendid athlete was now lying there where a few minutes ago there was nothing. Yahweh spoke:

"Remember in the Old Testament this description in Ezekiel 37:

'Son of man, can these bones live? . . . there was a noise, and behold a shaking, and the bones came together, bone to his bone. And when I beheld, lo, the sinews and the flesh came up upon them, and the skin covered them above . . . and the breath came into them, and they lived, and stood up upon their feet, an exceeding great army.' (Ezekiel 37: 3, 7, 8, 10)

The description which you will make would

*added in translation

certainly be close to the one of Ezekiel, apart from the noise which we have been able to remove."

Indeed, what I had seen corresponded perfectly with Ezekiel's description. Then, the person lying down slid to the left and disappeared completely out of my sight. A trap door opened, and I saw the creature whose creation I had witnessed in a few minutes, lying on a very white fabric. He was still immobile, but suddenly he opened his eyes and got up, came down a few steps to our level, and after having exchanged a few words with another robot, came towards me. There, he gave me his hand which I shook, and I felt his skin soft and warm.

Yahweh asked me :

"Do you have a picture of a loved one with you?"

"Yes, I have the picture of my mother in my wallet, which remained in my clothes."

He showed it to me and asked me if it was the right one. As I said yes, he gave it to one of the robots who inserted it in the machine and touched some parts of the system. In front of the window, I witnessed a new fabrication of a living being. Then when the skin started to cover the flesh, I realised what was happening: They were going to make an exact replica of my mother, from the picture I had furnished . . . . Indeed, a few moments later, I was able to kiss my mother or rather the image of my mother as she was ten years ago, for the picture I had given was about ten years old. Yahweh said to me:

"Now allow us to make a small injection on your forehead."

One of the robots came towards me and with the help of a small apparatus similar to a syringe, made an injection in my forehead which I hardly felt as it was so light. Then he inserted the syringe into the enormous machine and touched other parts of the machine. Again a being was being formed under my very eyes. When the skin covered the flesh, I saw another me taking shape little by little. Indeed, the being that came out of the machine was an exact replica of myself. Yahweh told me:

"As you can see, this other you doesn't have a small stone on his forehead which is characteristic of the robots and which the replica of your mother had. From a photo, we can only make a replica of the physical body, with no psychical personality or almost none, whereas from a cell like the one which we sampled from betweeen your eyes, we can make a total replica of the individual whose cell we sampled with their memory, personality, and character. We could now send the other you back to Earth and people would not notice anything. We are going to destroy this replica immediately, for it is of no use to us. But at the moment, there are two yous who are listening to me, but the two personalities are becoming different, because you know you are going to live and he knows he is to be destroyed but that does not bother him because he knows he is nothing but yourself. This is another proof, if needed, of the non-existence of the soul, or of a purely spiritual entity peculiar to each body which certain primitives believe in."

We then left the room where the enormous machine was, then, through a corridor we entered another hall where there were other installations. We approached another machine.

"In this machine are kept the cells of malevolent people who will be recreated to be judged when the time comes. All those on Earth who preached violence, wickedness, aggressiveness, and obscurantism, who although they had all the elements at hand to understand where they came from but were not able to recognize the truth, will be recreated, to undergo the punishment which they deserve after being judged by those whom they made suffer or by their ancestors or descendants.

You now well deserve a little rest. This robot will be your guide and will furnish you with anything you desire until tomorrow morning, and then we will again have some things to say to you and then we shall accompany you back to Earth. You will have from now until then a foretaste of what awaits you when your mission will be over on your planet."

Then I saw a robot coming towards me and he saluted me respectfully. He was very tall, very handsome, and dark with a beardless and sporty type of face.

A Foretaste of Paradise

The robot asked me if I wanted to see my room and after I agreed, he handed me a belt used for travelling. I found myself being transported above the ground again and when I was back in contact with the ground, I was in front of a house looking more like a scallop shell than a residence. The interior was entirely carpeted with shaggy furs and a huge bed, at least as big as four earth beds, and was like sunken in the ground, recognizable only by the different colour of the furs covering it. In a corner of the huge room, a huge bathtub, also sunken in the ground, and as big as a swimming pool, was installed among vegetation of marvellous shapes and colours.

"Would you like some female companious?" asked the robot. "Come, you will make your choice."

I put my belt back on, and I found myself transported in front of the machine used for fabricating the robots. A luminous cube appeared in front of me. I was told to sit in an armchair facing the cube and was given a helmet. When I had settled down, a magnificent young brunette, with marvellously harmonious proportions, appeared in three dimensions within the luminous cube. She moved in such a way so as to show herself off, and had she not been in a cube floating one meter (3.3 ft*) above the ground, I would have really thought she was real. My robot

*added in translation

asked me whether she pleased me or if I would like to have her shape altered or her face modified. I told him that I found her perfect. He replied that aesthetically speaking she was the ideal woman or rather one of the three types of ideal woman as defined by the computer in relation to the taste of the majority of residents of the planet, but that I could ask for any modification that I wished. Following my refusal to change anything whatsoever about that magnificent creature, a second woman, blond and heady this time, appeared in the luminous cube, different but just as perfect as the first one. I couldn't find anything to alter there either. Finally a third young person more sensual than the first two and red haired this time, appeared in the strange cube. The robot asked me if I wanted to see other models or if these three ideal types from my race would suffice. Of course I answered that I thought these beings were extraordinary.

At that moment, a magnificent black woman appeared in the cube, then a very slender and slim Chinese woman, and then a young voluptuous oriental woman. The robot asked me which person I desired to have as a companion. Since I answered that they all pleased me, he went towards the robot making machine and spoke for a moment with one of his peers. Then the machine was set in motion and I understood what was about to happen.

A few minutes later, I was back in my residence with my six companions. There, I had the most unforgettable bath that I have ever had, in the company of those charming robots, absolutely submissive to all my desires. Then my robot guide asked me if I wished to make some music. Following my affirmative reply, he took out a helmet similar to the one I had put on before the projection of the feminine robot models. The robot asked me: "Now imagine some music that you would like to hear." Immediately a sound corresponding exactly to the music that I had been thinking about could be heard, and as I constructed a melody in my head, that melody became reality with sounds of an amplitude and a sensitivity that were more extraordinary than any I had ever heard before. The dream of every composer had become a reality: the ability to compose music directly without having to go through the laborious process of writing and orchestrating.

Then my six adorable companions began dancing to my music in a most voluptuous and bewitching way.

After a while, my robot asked me if I would also like to compose images. Another helmet was given to me and I sat in front of a semi-circular screen. I then started imagining some scenes and these scenes became visible on the screen. It was in fact an immediate visualization of all the thoughts that could come to me. I started thinking about my grandmother and she appeared on the screen. I thought of a bouquet of flowers and it appeared and if I imagined a rose with green spots on, it would appear too. This apparatus enabled one to instantaneously visualize one's thought without having to explain them. What a marvel. My robot told me:

"With training, one can create a story and play it out. Many performances of this kind, performances of direct creation, are held here."

Finally after a while I went to bed and spent the most extravagant night of my life with my marvellous female companions.

The next day, I got up, took another perfumed bath, and then a robot served us a delicious breakfast. Then he asked me to follow him, for Yahweh was expecting me. I put the transportation belt on and soon found myself in front of a strange machine where the president of the council of eternals was waiting for me. It was not as big as the one that creates robots but it was still very big. In its center was a large embedded armchair. Yahweh asked me if I had had a pleasant night, and then explained to me:

"This machine will awaken certain faculties which are dormant in you. Your brain will then be able to exploit its full potential. Sit down here."

I sat in the chair which he pointed me to and a sort of shell covered my skull. I thought I was losing consciousness for a moment and then it felt as if my head was about to explode. I could see multicolored flashes passing in front of my eyes. Finally, everything stopped and a robot helped me out of the armchair. I felt terribly different. I had the impression that everything was simple and easy. Yahweh spoke:

"From now on, we will see through your eyes, hear through your ears and speak through your mouth. We will even be able to heal through your hands, as we already do at Lourdes and in many other places of the world, certain sick people whom we judge deserve that we do something for them because of their will to radiate the messages we have given you, and by their effort to acquire a cosmic mind by opening themselves to infinity. We observe everyone. Huge computers assure a constant surveillance of all people living on Earth. A mark is attributed to everyone depending on their actions during their life whether they walked towards love and truth or towards hate and obscurantism. When the time for evaluating comes, those who went in the right direction will be allowed eternity on this paradisiac planet, those who were not evil without having achieved anything positive will not be recreated and for those who were particularly negative, a cell from their body is preserved, so that we may recreate them when the time comes, in order that they be judged and serve punishment they deserve.

You, who are reading this message, understand clearly that you can have access to this marvellous world, to this paradise. You will be welcome, you who follow our messenger, Claude Rael, our ambassador on the road to universal love and cosmic harmony, you who will help him realize what we will ask of him, for we see through his eyes, hear through his ears and speak through his mouth.

Your idea of creating a congregation of guides for humanity is very good. But be strict with regard to their selection so that our message is neither deformed nor betrayed.

Meditation is indispensable for opening one's mind,

but asceticism is useless. You must enjoy life with all the strength of your senses, for the wakening of the senses goes together with the wakening of the mind. Continue to do sport if you wish and if you have the time, for all sports and games are good, since they develop musculature or better still, self-control, such as car sports or motorbikes.

When a person feels alone, he can always try to communicate telepathically with us, while still trying to be in harmony with infinity; he will feel an immense well-being. What you have advised concerning a gathering of people who believe in us in each region on Sunday morning at about eleven o'clock is very good. Few members are presently doing so.

Medium are useful, seek them, but balance them for their gift of mediumship (which is only a telepathic gift) unbalances them and they begin to believe in the 'supernatural', in magic and other things which are just as stupid, such as believing in an etheric body, a new way of believing in a soul which doesn't exist!!! In fact they are merely tuning into people who lived several centuries ago and whom we recreated on this paradisiac planet.

There is an important revelation that you may make now: The Jews are our direct descendants on Earth. That's why a specific destiny is reserved for them. They are the descendants of the sons of Elohim and daughters of men, as mentioned in Genesis. The original mistake of these sons of Elohim was to have mated with their scientific creations, the daughters of men. That is why their descendants have suffered for such a long time. But for them the time of forgiveness has come and they will now be able to live peacefully in their recovered country unless they make another mistake of not recognizing you as our messenger. We hope that our embassy on Earth will be built in Israel on a piece of land which the government will give you. If they refuse, you may build it elsewhere and Israel will undergo a new chastisement for not having recognized our messenger.

You must devote yourself only to your mission. Dont't worry, you will be able to support your family. People who believe in you and therefore in us will help you. You are our messenger, our ambassador, our prophet and in any case, you have your place reserved here among all the other prophets. You are the one who must gather together people from all religions. For the movement you have created, the Raelian Movement, must be the religion of religions. I insist, it is indeed a religion but an atheistic religion as you have already understood. And you are our ambassador, our prophet. We won't forget those who have helped you and we won't forget those who have caused you trouble either. Don't be afraid and fear no one for whatever happens, you have your place amongst us. Shake up a little those who lose confidence. Two thousand years ago, those who believed in our messenger Jesus were thrown into the den to the lions, today what do you risk? The irony of fools? The sneers of those who have understood nothing and prefer to keep their primitive beliefs?

What is all that compared to the lion's den? What is all that compared with what awaits those who will follow you? Truly it is easier than ever to follow one's intuition. In the Koran, Muhammad, who is among us, said on the subject of prophets:

"The moment for men to give account is drawing near; and yet in their nonchalance they are turning away (from their Creator)."

"No new warning comes from their Creator that they don't listen to laugh at."

"And their hearts are amused by it."

"Those who do evil comfort themselves secretly by saying:

'Is not this man only a mortal as we are? . . . .'

'It is a jumble of dreams. He made it all up himself. He is a poet!'

'But let him bring a miracle like those who were sent in the time past.' " (Koran, Surah 21:1 to 5)

Even Muhammad had to suffer the sarcasm of certain people, and Jesus suffered them too. When he was on the cross, some said:

"If thou be the Son of God, come down from the cross." (Matthew 27:40)

And yet as you have seen, Jesus is in marvellous shape and for eternity, as is Muhammad and all those who followed and believed in them, whereas those who have criticized them will be recreated for their chastisement.

The computers which follow the people who have no knowledge of the messages are linked to a system which automatically from a distance samples a cell at the time of death from which they may be recreated, if they deserve it.

While waiting to build our embassy, create a monastery near where you live for the Guides of MADECH. You who are our prophet, the Guide of Guides, will be able to train there, those who will be in charge of radiating our messages all over the Earth.

The New Commandments

Those who wish to follow you will apply the laws I am now about to give you:

'You will appear at least once in your life before the Guide of Guides so that he may trnasmit through manual contact, or through an initiated guide, your cellular plan to the computer which will take this into account at the time of judgement when weighing up your life.'

'You will think at least once a day about the Elohim, your Creators.'

'You will try by all means to radiate the Elohim's message around you.'

'At least once a year, you will give a donation to the Guide of Guides equal to at least one percent of your annual income in order to help him to devote his full time to his mission and to travel around the world to spread this message.'

'At least once a year, you will invite the Guide of your region to your home and you will gather at your place people who are interested in hearing him explain the dimensions of the message.'

In the event that the Guide of Guides disappears, the new Guide of Guides will be designated by the former Guide of Guides. The Guide of Guides will be the guardian of the embassy of the Elohim on Earth and will be able to live there with his family and with the people of his choice.

You, Claude Rael, you are our ambassador on Earth and the people who believe in you must provide you with the means to accomplish your mission. You are the last of the prophets before the Judgement, you are the prophet of the religion of religions, the demystifier and the shepherd of shepherds. You are the one whose coming was announced in all the religions by the ancient prophets, our representatives. You are the one who will bring back the shepherds' flocks before the water is spilled, the one who will bring back the created to their Creators, those who have ears can hear, those who have eyes can see. All those who have their eyes open will see that you are the first prophet who can be understood by scientifically evolved people only. All that you tell is incomprehensible to primitive people. This is a sign that will be noticed by those whose eyes are open, the sign of the revelation, of the apocalypse.

To The People of Israel

The State of Israel must give a territory situated near Jerusalem to the Guide of Guides so that he may build the residence, the embassy of the Elohim. The time has come, people of Israel, to build the new

Jerusalem as was foreseen. Claude Rael is the announced one, reread your writings and open your eyes.

We wish to have our embassy among our descendants since the people of Israel are the descendants of the children born out of the unions between the sons of Elohim and the daughters of men.

People of Israel, we took you out of the claws of the Egyptians and you did not show yourselves worthy of our confidence, we entrusted you with a message destined for the whole of humanity and you jealously kept it instead of spreading it, you have long suffered for your errors but the time of forgiveness has come, and as foreseen we have said 'to the North give and to the South do not hold back'. I gathered your sons and daughters from the ends of the earth, as Isaiah had written, and you have been able to find your country again, you will be able to live there in peace if you listen to the last of the prophets, the one who was announced to you, and if you help accomplish what we ask of him.

This is your last chance, otherwise another country will welcome the Guide of Guides and build our embassy on its territory, and that country will be close to yours, it will be protected and happiness shall prevail, and the State of Israel will be destroyed once more.

You, son of Israel, who has not yet returned to the ancestral grounds, wait before returning there to see if the government will accept that our embassy be built there. If it is refused, do not return, and you will be one of those who will be saved from the destruction and whose descendants will be able one day to find the promised land again, when the time comes.

People of Israel, recognize the one announced to you, give him the territory to build our embassy, and help him build it. Otherwise, as happened 2,000 years ago, it will be constructed elsewhere, and if it is constructed elsewhere, you will be dispersed again.

If two thousand years ago, you had recognized that Jesus was indeed our messenger, all the Christians in the world would not be Christians but Jews, you would not have had problems, and you would have remained our ambassadors, but instead this task was given to other men who took Rome for their base. Two thousand years ago, you did not recognize our messenger and it was not Jerusalem but Rome that shone. Now you have a new chance for it to be Jerusalem once more, and if you do not grab it, another country will shelter our embassy and you will no longer be allowed the land we had chosen for you.

There, I have finished. You will be able to annotate all this by yourself once on Earth. Now, enjoy this paradise a while longer, and we will take you back for you to complete your mission before returning back to us for good."

I remained there for several more hours, enjoying the many pleasures of that world, wandering among numerous fountains and devoting myself to the company of the great prophets whom I had met the day before during the meditation sessions.

Then after a last meal taken with the same people as the day before, I was once again in the large vessel which put me down in the observation station. From there, I followed the same circuit as the day before, and found myself with my clothes in the small vessel which put me down where it had picked me up, at Roc Plat. I looked at my watch: it was midnight. I returned home where I immediately set to work writing all that had been told to me. Everything was perfectly clear in my mind and I was surprised to notice that I was writing it all in one stroke without hesitating to recall the sentences I had heard. The words had remained as if engraved in my mind, as I had been told at the beginning.

When I had finished narrating what had happened to me, I began to feel clearly that something in me was set in motion which had never happened to me before and I began writing while observing all that I was writing and discovering it as a reader. I was writing, but I didn't feel like the author of what was appearing on the paper. The Elohim were starting to speak through my mouth, or rather, to write with my hand. And what was being written under my eyes concerned all the subjects a person is confronted with during his life and the proper way to behave when faced with these problems. It was in fact a code of life, a new way of behaving faced with life's events, of behaving as a human, that is to say as an evolved being, and therefore trying in every way to open one's mind to infinity and to place oneself in harmony with it. These great rules dictated by the

Elohim, our Creators, our fathers who are in heaven, as our ancestors used to say without quite understanding are all here, expressed in their integrality.

CHAPTER 3
THE KEYS

Introduction
Man
Birth
Education
Sensual Education
Fulfilment
Society, The Government
Meditation and Prayer
The Arts
Sensual Meditation
Human Justice
Science
The Human Brain
The Apocalypse
Telepathic Communication
The Reward
The Guides

INTRODUCTION

These writings are the keys which enable us to open our minds which thousands of years of obscurantism have locked up, imprisoned as a fossil.

The door which locks up the human mind is blocked by many locks which must all be opened at the same time if one wants the mind to come out towards infinity. If only one key is used, the other bolts will remain blocked and if they are not all kept open at the same time, then while the second is being opened, the first one will close again thus preventing the opening. Human society is afraid of what it cannot understand, therefore it is afraid of what is behind this door, even if it is happiness through the access of truth. Therefore, society applies pressure too to prevent certain people from half-opening this door and prefers to remain in its misfortune and its ignorance. It is yet another obstacle on the threshold of the door through which the mind can free itself. But as Gandhi said: "it is not because no one sees the truth that it becomes an error", and so if you attempt to open this door, ignore the sarcasm of those who have seen nothing or those who have seen but pretend not to see anything because of their fear of the unknown. And if the opening of the door seems too difficult for you, ask for the help of the guides, for the guides have already opened the door of their mind and they know of the difficulties involved. They will not be able to open your door for you but they will be able to explain to you the different techniques which will enable you to succeed. Besides, they are living witnesses of the happiness caused by the opening of the door, and the proof that those who are afraid of what is behind it, are wrong.

Man

In all cases, we must always consider things according to four levels, first of all:

–in relation to infinity;

–in relation to the Elohim, our fathers, our Creators;

–in relation to human society;

–finally, in relation to the individual.

The most important level is the one in relation to infinity, it is in relation to this level that everything must be judged but with a constant: love, therefore taking into account others who must be given love, for one must live in harmony with infinity, therefore with others who are a part of infinity too.

Then we must take into accout the advice given by the Elohim, our Creators, and to act in such a way that human society listens to the advice of those who begot it.

Then, we must take into account society, which has enabled, enables and will enable men to blossom on the path of truth. It must be taken into account but not followed, on the contrary, society must be helped to emerge from its primitive state of encrusted and fossilised conventions by questioning all its habits and traditions, even if they are supported by laws, laws that try only to lock up minds in the yoke of obscurantism.

Finally, one must take into accout the blossoming of the individual without which the mind does not reach its full potential, and without which it is not possible to be in harmony with infinity and to become a new human being.

Birth

You will never impose any religion on a child, who is still but a larva, unable to understand what is happening to him. Therefore, he must not be baptized, nor circumcised, nor made to undergo any act he would not have accepted. One must therefore wait for him to be old enough to understand and choose, and if by then a religion appeals to him, he should be allowed to adhere to it freely.

A birth should be a festivity, for the Elohim have created us in their image, therefore capable of reproducing by ourselves, and by creating a living being, we preserve the species which we are, and respect the work of our Creators.

A birth should be a festivity and an act of love, accomplished in harmony, as far as sound, colors or temperature are concerned so that the being who comes into contact with life gets into the habit of harmony.

On the other hand, one must immediately get him into the habit of respecting the liberty of others and when he cries at night, one must come to see him discreetly but without his ever realizing that his crying brings him a certain comfort due to being looked after. On the contrary, one must come to see and look after him when he says nothing and not come to see him (otherwise do so without his being aware of it) when he cries. Thus, he will get used to everything going better when he is in harmony with everything around him. "Help yourself and Heaven will help you (God helps those who help themselves*)."

In fact parents must understand as soon as it is born, that a child is first of all an individual and that no individual should be treated like a child.

Even our Creators do not treat us like children but as individuals, that is why they do not intervene directly to help us solve our problems, but leave us to overcome the obstacles we come across by our own reflection as responsible individuals.

Education

The little being who is still nothing but the "larva" of a man must, in its infancy, be accustomed to respect the liberty and the tranquility of others. Since he is too young to understand and to reason, corporal punishment should be sternly applied by the person who brings up the child, so that he suffers when he makes others suffer, or when he disturbs them by

*The English version of the proverb added in translation.

lacking respect. This corporal punishment should only be applied with very young children, and then, gradually as the child reasons and comprehends, should disappear progressively and eventually, disappear completely. From the age of seven, corporal punishment should be very exceptional and from the age of fourteen, it should never be applied.

You will use corporal punishment only for punishing the child for not respecting the freedom of others and yourself.

You will teach your child to blossom and you will teach him to always have a questioning attitude towards what society and its schools want to inculcate. You will not force him to learn things which are no use to him at all and you will let him take the orientation which he wishes, because don't forget that the most important thing is his fulfilment.

You will teach him always to judge things successively in relation to infinity, in relation to our Creators, in relation to society, and in relation to himself.

You will not impose any religion on your child but you will teach him without prejudice, the various beliefs which exist throughout the world, or at least the most important ones in chronological order: Jewish religion, Christian religion and Muslim religion. If you can, try to learn about the major lines of oriental religions in order to be able to explain them to your child. Finally, you will explain to him the main points of the message given by the Elohim to the last of the prophets.

You will teach him above all to love the world in

which he lives, and through this world, our Creators.

You will teach him to open himself to infinity and to try to live in harmony with infinity.

You will teach him the marvellous work accomplished by the Elohim, our Creators, you will teach him always to think and research so that men may one day be capable of doing again what their Creators have done, that is to say, of scientifically creating other humanities elsewhere.

You will teach him to consider himself as a part of infinity, that is to say, very much and very little. "From dust were ye made and dust ye shall become."

You will teach him that the wrong done to others cannot be made up for by any confession, or any absolution once it is done and it must not be believed that it is sufficient to begin, when death is near, to believe in any god or the Elohim, to have the right to eternity.

You will teach him that we are judged by what we do right throughout our life and that the path which leads to wisdom is long and that it takes a whole lifetime to engage ourselves sufficiently. He who has not followed the right direction during his whole life, will not have the right to scientific resurrection on the planet of eternals just because he makes a sudden change in the right direction. That is unless his regret is sincere and he acts with intensity in the right direction making up for lost time and trying to be forgiven by those to whom he has done wrong and trying to devote all his means to bring them love and happiness. And that will still not be sufficient for the one who made others suffer. Because even if he is forgiven by them and if he gives them love, he will have simply succeeded in erasing his errors but he will have done nothing positive, he will then have to begin new actions, bringing happiness to people whom he has never harmed, and helping those who spread the truth, the guides. But it is too late for a being who regrets only at the moment of his death or shortly before, and he will not be pardoned.

Sensual Education

This is one of the most important things, and which at the moment, practically does not exist.

You will awaken the mind of your child, but you will also awaken his body, because the awakening of the body is linked with the awakening of the mind.

All those who seek to numb the body are also numbing the mind.

Our Creators have given us senses for us to use. The nose is meant to smell, the eyes to see, the ears to hear, the mouth to taste and the fingers to touch. We must develop our senses in order to enjoy more all that surrounds us and which our Creators placed here for us to enjoy.

A sensual being is much more likely to be in harmony with infinity because he feels it without having to meditate or reflect. Meditation and reflection will enable that being to better understand this harmony and to radiate it around him by teaching it.

To be sensual, means to let the environment in

which you exist give you pleasure. Sexual education is also very important but it only teaches the technical functions of organs and their usefulness, while sensual education must teach us how to get pleasure from our organs, purely for pleasure's sake; without necessarily seeking to use our organs for their utilitarian purpose only.

To say nothing to one's children about sex is wrong, and explaining to them what it is for is better but it is still not sufficient: it must be explained to them how they can use it for getting pleasure.

Explaining to them only "what it is for" is as if one tells them about music saying that it is for marching to, or other nonsense, or that knowing how to write is only for writing claim letters, or that cinema is only to give audio-visual courses. Fortunately, thanks to artists and by an awakening of the senses one can get pleasure by listening, reading or looking at works which were made for no other reason than to give pleasure. The same goes for the sexual organ. It is not just for satisfying our natural needs or for assuring reproduction but is also for giving pleasure to others and to oneself. Thanks to science, we have finally come out, of the times when showing one's body was a "sin", and when any copulation brought in itself its punishment: the conception of a child. Now, thanks to contraceptive techniques, sexual union is freely possible without it having to become a definite commitment or possibly being one. You will teach this to your child without shame but on the contrary, with love, clearly explaining that he is made to be happy and to blossom fully, that is to say, to enjoy life with all the force of his senses, of all his senses.

You will never be ashamed of your body or of your nudity, for nothing displeases our Creators more than to see those who were created feeling shame for the appearance which was given to them.

You will teach your children to love their bodies as we should love every part of the creation of the Eloḥim, because in loving their creation, we also love them.

Every one of our organs was created by our fathers, the Elohim, so that we might use them without feeling any shame and being happy using things which were designed to be used. And if the act of using one of these organs brings pleasure, it means that our Creators wished us to get pleasure using it.

Every man is a garden which should not remain uncultivated. A life without pleasure is like an uncultivated garden. Pleasure is the fertilizer which opens the mind. Asceticism is useless unless it is a temporary ordeal designed to train the mind to dominate the body. But once we have succeeded in the ordeal we have set, and which should always be limited in time, we should once more enjoy the pleasure of life. Asceticism can be accepted as the lying fallow of the garden which is a man. That is to say a momentary pause in the search for pleasure enabling us to better appreciate it later on.

You will accustom your children to have more and more freedom by considering them always and above all as individuals.

You will respect their inclinations and their tastes as you would like them to respect your inclinations and tastes. And make sure that you realize always that your child is what he is, and that you will not be able to make him what you want him to be, as he will not be able to make you what he wants you to be. Respect him so that he respects you, and respect his tastes so that he respect yours.

Fulfilment

An individual should try to fulfil himself according to his aspirations and tastes without worrying about what others think, as long as he does not do any harm to others.

If you feel like doing something, first check that it does not harm anyone, then do it without worrying about what others think of it.

If you feel like having a sensual or sexual experience with one or several other individuals whatever may be their sex, you may behave as you desire as long as this or these individuals agree.

All is permitted on the path of true fulfilment for the opening of the body, and therefore, of the mind.

We are at last emerging from the primitive times when women were considered to be merely reproductive organs belonging to society. Woman, thanks to science, can now freely and sensually experience fulfilment without having to fear the punishment of pregnancy. Woman, at last, is truly the equal of man, since she can truly enjoy her body without having the fear of enduring alone the undesired consequences of her acts.

The conception of a child is something too important to be left to chance.

When you conceive a child, you will do it while being aware of what you are doing and because you have chosen to do so, conceiving in a marvellous act of love having thoroughly thought about it beforehand and being sure of really wanting it. Because a child cannot be well conceived unless he was truly desired at the very moment of conception. The moment of conception is the most important moment because it is at that time that the first cell, therefore the plan of the individual is conceived, this moment must therefore be desired so that the first cell may be made in a perfect harmony, the two minds of the parents being conscious and strongly thinking of the being which they are conceiving. This is one of the secrets of the new man.

If you are only looking for the fulfilment of your body, therefore the blossoming of your mind, use the means which science offers you. To begin with, know about contraception. Only conceive a child when you yourself are fulfiled, so that the being you conceive may be the fruit of the union of two blossomed beings.

To reach fulfilment, use the means which science puts at your disposal, enabling you to open your body to pleasure without any risks. Pleasure and procreation are two different things which must not be confused. The first is for the individual, the second is for the species. It is only when the individual is fulfiled that he can create a fulfiled being.

If by mishap you have conceived a being without desiring it, use the means which science puts at your disposal: use abortion. Because a being which was not desired at the moment of conception cannot fully blossom because he was not created in harmony. Do not listen to those who try to frighten you by talking about the physical and especially the ethical after-effects which an abortion can cause. There aren't any if you have it done by competent people. On the contrary, it is the keeping of the undesired child which would leave you with physical and moral disturbances which would be passed on to the child you brought to the world and make it suffer too.

To have a child does not necessarily imply being married or even living with a man. Already, many women have decided to have one or more children without being married or living with a man. The education of a child, who is an individual right from birth, should not necessarily be given by the parents. It would often be more preferable for his education to be entrusted to specialized people who would contribute far more than certain parents towards their children's fulfilment.

If you wish to have a child without living with a man, do as you wish. Filfil yourself as you wish, without worrying what others think.

And if you choose to do this, don't think that you are condemned because of this to live alone for ever:

welcome the men you like and they will serve as masculine models for your child. And you can even decide one day to live with a man, this will not cause any problem for your child but will contribute to his fulfilment. A change of environment is always positive for a child.

Society should organize itself to take charge of the education of children partially or totally depending on the parents' wishes. Those who want to work should be able to leave their children in the custody of competent people, and those who want their children to receive an education given entirely by competent people, should be able to completely entrust their children in the establishment arranged for this purpose.

Thus, if you give birth to a child you desired, but after his birth you are separated from your companion, or for any other reason, and you no longer desire the child, you will be able to entrust him to society so that he may be brought up in the harmony necessary for his fulfilment. For a child who grows up in an environment where he is not really or intensely desired cannot blossom and be fulfiled.

A child is a mutual fulfilment. If the child becomes a nuisance, however slightly, he realizes it and his fulfilment is affected. He should therefore be kept near you only if his presence is felt as a fulfilment. If not, he should be put in establishments that society must build to allow him to fulfil himself and put there without the least regret but on the contrary, with a profound joy which should be that of the person who entrusts their child to people who will be more capable than they themselves in bringing forth the blossoming and fulfilment of the little being.

Regular visits can even take place if the child, whose wishes are of primary consideration, would like them. The people in charge of their education should always describe the parents to the children as exceptional people since they placed more importance on their children's fulfilment than on their own selfish pleasure of bringing them up themselves, by entrusting them to people more competent than they are.

You will therefore freely choose your partner if you desire one. Marriage, whether it be religious or civil, is useless. One cannot sign a contract as if one were selling oil, when it is a matter of uniting living beings, who are sure to change because they are living.

You will reject marriage which is only the proclamation of ownership of a person. A man or a woman cannot be the property of anyone else. Any contract can only destroy the harmony existing between two beings. When one feels loved, one feels free to love, but when one has signed a contract, one feels like a prisoner, forced to love and sooner or later, each one begins to hate the other.

You will live with the person of your choice for only as long as you feel good with them.

When you no longer get on well together, do not remain together because your union would become hell. All living beings evolve and rightly so. If the personal evolution of each individual is similar, the unions last, but if their progress is different, then the unions are no longer possible. The being whom you used to like, now no longer pleases you because you (or he) have changed. You must part from each other while keeping a good memory of your union instead of spoiling it with useless bickering which gives way to aggression. To begin with, a child chooses the clothes which fit him but when he outgrows them and the clothes are too small for him, he must take them off so as to put on others, otherwise he will end up by tearing them to pieces.

Above all, don't be worried about your child, it is better for him to be with only one of his parents in harmony than being with the two in discord or without a perfect harmony. For don't forget that children are above all individuals.

Society must absolutely ensure that old people have a happy life without any material worries.

But although we must respect the aged and do everything for their happiness, we must not listen to them just because of their seniority. An intelligent man can give good advice whatever his age, but a stupid person, even if he is a hundred years old, does not deserve to be listened to for even one second, and whats more, he has no excuse, for he has had his whole life in which to try to awaken himself whereas there is still hope for a young and stupid person. But in any case, a stupid old man must be able to live comfortably. It is the duty of society.

Death should not be an occasion of sad meetings but on the contrary, a joyful celebration because it is the moment when the beloved one may perhaps reach the paradise of the eternals in the company of the Elohim, our Creators.

You will ask therefore not to be buried religiously, but you will donate your body to science or you will ask that your body be disposed of as discreetly as possible, except for the bone of your forehead, more precisely the part located above the beginning of the nose, 33 mm (1.3 in*) above the middle of the axis linking your two pupils. There must be at least one square centimeter (0.4 in square*) of this bone which you will have sent to the Guide of Guides so that he may keep it in our terrestrial embassy. Because each person is watched by a computer which notes and will take score of his actions at the end of his life, but the people who know about the messages which Claude Rael transmitted, will be recreated from the cells which they will have left in our embassy. For them, this recreation will take place only if they send the required part of their body to the Guide of Guides after their death, for as soon as they know about the message, the mechanism within the computer which records the information to be used for the judgement will remain in operation but the one which enables an automatic sampling of a cell at the moment of death is disconnected, for only those who apply exactly what is required once they know about the message will be thus recreated.

You will have made sure that you see at least once

*added in translation

in your life the Guide of Guides or a guide qualified by him to transmit your cellular plan to the Elohim so that they may awaken your mind and help you to remain awakened.

In compliance with what is written in the Book, you will not leave any inheritance to your children, apart from the apartment or the family house. The rest, you will leave by will to the Guide of Guides and if you fear that your descendants might not respect your last will by trying to recover your property through human justice, you will bestow it while you are alive to the Guide of Guides in order to help him spread the Messages of our Creators on Earth.

And you who remain, do not be sad and do not lament after the death of a loved one. Try instead to give love to those you love while they are still living, because once they are dead, what makes you unhappy is the thought that perhaps you had not loved the departed one enough and that now it is too late.

If he was good, he has the right to the Elohim's gardens for eternity, and he knows happiness, and if he has not been good, he does not deserve to be missed.

Anyway, even if he is not among those chosen, he does not really vanish. Death is not a very important thing, and we should not be afraid of death. It is just like falling asleep, except it's an endless sleep.

And since we are a part of infinity, the matter of which we are made does not disappear. It continues to exist in the soil, in plants, or even in animals, but obviously, losing all homogenity and therefore, all identity. But this part of infinity which had been organized by our Creators according to a very precise structure, returns to infinity while remaining a part of this small ball called the Earth, and which is alive.

Everyone has the right to life, the right to love, and the right to death. Everyone is the master of his life and of his death. Death is nothing, but suffering is terrible and everything must be done to remove it. A being who suffers too much has the right to commit suicide. If he has been good during his life, he will be admitted to the planet of the eternals.

If a person you love suffers very much and wishes to die without having the strength to commit suicide, help him to kill himself.

When, thanks to science, men will be able to remove the suffering of their fellow men, they will then be able to ask themselves whether it is right or not to commit suicide.

Society

The Government

It is indispensable that there is a government which makes decisions, just as in the human body there is a brain which makes them.

You will do all that is possible to set up a government practicing Geniocracy which places intelligence in power.

You will participate in the creation of a world Humanitarian party advocating humanitarianism and geniocracy as described in the First Message, and you will support its candidates.

Only geniocracy can enable men to fully reach the golden age.

Total democracy is not good. A body in which all the cells command cannot survive. Only the intelligent people should be able to make decisions involving mankind. Therefore, you will refuse to vote, unless a candidate advocating geniocracy and humanitarianism appears.

Neither universal suffrage nor Gallup polls are valid for governing the world. To govern is to foresee and not to follow the reactions of a sheep-like people, of which only a very small part is sufficiently awakened to guide mankind. Since there are very few awakened people, then if we were to base the decisions on universal suffrage or opinion polls the decisions made would be the choice of the majority, therefore of those who are not awakened, and who react according to their immediate satisfaction or as a result of their instinctive reactions buried unconsciously in their gangue of their obscurantist conditioning.

Only geniocracy which is a selective democracy is worthwhile. As it is stated in the First Message, only the people whose net level of intelligence is 50% superior to the average should be eligible and only those whose net level of intelligence is 10% superior to the average may be electors. Scientists are already developing techniques which will enable us to measure net intelligence. Listen to their advice and act in a way such that the most precious mineral of mankind the exceptionally gifted children, may receive an education at a level comparable to their genius, for a normal education is designed for normal children, which means, only for children with average intelligence.

It is not the number of diplomas that you've managed to get which counts, since this only calls upon the rather uninteresting faculty of memory, which machines can replace. Intelligence in its raw state is what can make peasants or workers much more intelligent than engineers or professors. This can be compared to common sense, to the creative genius, for most inventions are nothing but a question of common sense.

To govern is to foresee and all the big problems which mankind is now facing prove that governments did not foresee and therefore were unable to govern. It is not a problem of people but a problem of the technique used to choose who is to be made responsible. It is the way we select our governors which is not good. Random democracy must be replaced by selective democracy: geniocracy, which puts intelligent people in power. That is not much to ask for.

Human laws are indispensable and you will respect them in such a way that those which are unfair or obsolete are changed.

Between human laws and those of our Creators, you will not hesitate an instant. For even human judges will be judged some day by our Creators.

Police are indispensable as long as man has not yet discovered the medical way of eradicating violence and preventing criminals or those who infringe upon other people's freedom from acting as such.

As opposed to soldiers, who are the keepers of war, policemen are the keepers of peace and are temporarily indispensable for as long as science has not solved this problem.

You will refuse military service and request to be granted the status of conscientious objector which enables you to do your service in a division which does not carry weapons, as is your right if your religious or philosophical convictions forbid you to kill your fellow-men and which is the case for those who believe in the Elohim, our Creators, and want to follow the directives of the Guide of Guides of Madech. Contrary to what many young people think, conscientious objectors are not sent to jail but must work in civilian service or in a particular service where they do not carry weapons but for a period which is twice as long as the normal period of military service. It is better to spend two years in offices than to be trained for one year in techniques which enable you to kill your fellow-men.

Military service must be removed as soon as possible in all the countries of the world. All the professional armies should be transformed into guardians of world peace, that is to say, to be put at the service of freedom and human rights.

The only system which is worthwhile is that of geniocracy applying humanitarianism.

Capitalism is wrong, because it enslaves man to money and forces him into the profit of some on the backs of others.

Communism is wrong also, since it places more importance on equality than liberty. There should be equality between man at the beginning, at birth, but not after. Although all men have the right to live decently, those who work more than others for their fellow-men have the right to get more than those who do nothing for the community.

This is obviously a temporary rule, until man is capable of having all labour accomplished by robots so that he can devote himself exclusively to his fulfilment, after having totally abolished money.

In the meantime, it is shameful that while some people are dying of hunger, others throw away food so that prices do not collapse. Instead of throwing away this food, they should distribute it to those who have nothing to eat.

Work should not be considered as something sacred. Everyone has the right to be comfortably off even if he does not work. Everyone should try to fulfil himself and blossom in the field which attracts him. If men organize themselves, it will not take them long to mechanize and automate entirely all indispensable work. Then they will be able to blossom and fulfil themselves freely.

If all men really set themselves to it, it will only be a few years before men are relieved from the obligation of working. What is needed, is that in a marvelous burst of enthusiasm and solidarity for the liberation of mankind from material constraints, all technical and scientific capacities and all workers, truly set their minds to working intensely for the entire community and for its well being, rather than for vested interests, using all the means that are wasted on military budgets or for other silly things such as the realization of atomic weapons or of space flights which would be better planned and much more easily done, once man is free of material constraints. You have computers and electronic equipment which can replace man for the better. Use all this in order that these technical means be really at the service of mankind. In a few years, you could build a totally different world. You have arrived at the golden age.

Do everything to create the biological robot which will relieve you from menial labor and enable you to blossom and fulfil yourselves.

Urbanism must be considered as described in the First Message. Men must build very tall communal houses, situated in the open country so that individual houses will not "eat up" nature. Never forget that if every man has his country house with a small garden, there will be no more countryside. These communal houses must contain whole cities and include everything that a person needs. They must each be able to accomodate about fifty thousand inhabitants.

Man must respect nature for as long as he is not capable of recreating it, and for as long as he is not capable of becoming a Creator himself. By respecting nature, you respect those who created it, our fathers, the Elohim. You will never make animals suffer. You may kill them to feed on their flesh but without making them suffer. For although death is nothing, suffering is an abomination and you must avoid animals suffering as you must prevent men from suffering.

Nevertheless do not eat too much meat and you will feel better for it.

You may live on all that the land provides you with. You are not obliged to follow a special diet, you may eat meat, vegetables, fruits, plants and animals. It is stupid to follow a vegetarian diet under the pretext that you do not want to live on the meat of other living creatures. Plants, too, are alive and suffer in the same way as you do.

You will not cause plants to suffer, which are alive just as you are.

You will not intoxicate yourself with alcoholic beverages. You may drink a little wine when eating, for it is a product of the earth, but never intoxicate yourself. Exceptionally, you may drink alcoholic beverages, but in minute quantities and accompanied with solid food in order not to get drunk. Because a man who is drunk is no longer capable of being in harmony with infinity nor is he able to control himself and this is something lamentable in the eyes of our Creators.

You will not smoke, for the human body is not made to inhale smoke. This has lamentable effects on the organism and prevents total fulfilment and harmonisation with infinity.

You will not take drugs, you will not dope yourself, for the awakened mind needs nothing to come near to infinity: It is an abomination in the eyes of our Creators to see that men think they must take drugs to improve themselves. Man has no need to improve himself because he is perfect, for he is made in the image of the Creators. To say that man is imperfect is to insult our Creators who created us in their image. Man is perfect but he becomes resigned to this thought. An effort of each moment to keep oneself in a stage of awakening enables man to remain perfect, that is to say, just as we were created by the Elohim.

Meditation and Prayer

You will oblige yourself to meditate every day at least once, that is to say, to place yourself in relation to infinity, in relation to the Elohim, in relation to society and in relation to yourself.

You will meditate when you wake up so that your whole being will be perfectly conscious of infinity, in order to be in full possession of its means.

You will meditate before each meal in order that all your body may eat when you eat; and when you nourish yourself, you will think of what you are doing.

Your meditation will not be a dry meditation, but on the contrary, a sensual meditation. You will let yourself be overrun by peace and harmony until it becomes a pleasurable delight.

Your meditation should not be a forced labor but a pleasure. It is better not to meditate than to meditate without desiring it.

Don't impose meditation on your children or your neighbors but explain to them the pleasure that it provides and the well-being it gives, and if then they feel like meditating, try to teach them what you know.

You will think intensely of the Elohim, our Creators, at least once a day and try to correspond with them telepathically. Thus you will rediscover the original meaning of prayer. If you do not know how to do it you can inspire yourself from Our Father whose wordings are perfectly applicable for communication with our Creators.

You will make an attempt at telepathic communication in a group with the other people from your region who believe in the Elohim and with a Guide if possible, at least once a week.

You will do your best to attend the meeting every year of all those who believe in the Elohim and in the Messages they gave to the last of the prophets.

Technique for Attempting the Telepathic Contact with the Elohim

Here is a model of what you could say to be done while intensely thinking about the words and while looking at the sky.

Elohim, you are there somewhere near those stars,
Elohim, you are there and I know you are watching us,
Elohim, you are there and I would like so much to meet you,
Elohim, you are there and what am I to hope to deserve a contact,
Elohim, I recognize you as our Creators and I humbly place myself at your service,
Elohim, I recognize Claude Rael, your messenger, as my guide and I believe in him and in the message you have given him,
Elohim, I will do my best to make them known to those around me because I know I have not done enough,
Elohim, I love all human beings as my brothers because they are made in your image,
Elohim, I am trying to bring them happiness by opening their minds to infinity and by revealing to them what was revealed to me,
Elohim, I am trying to stop their suffering by putting my entire being at the service of mankind of which I am a part,
Elohim, I am trying to use as much as possible the mind you have given me, to enable mankind to emerge from darkness and suffering,
Elohim, I hope that you will judge the little I will have done by the end of my life to be sufficient for granting me the right to eternal life on the planet of the wise.

I love you as you must have loved man for admitting the best of them among your eternals.

The Arts

You will do your best to encourage artists and to help your child if he is attracted by the arts.

Art is one of the things wihich best enables you to become in harmony with infinity.

Consider every natural thing as an art and every art as a natural thing.

Surround yourself with artistic things, whether they appeal to the ears, to the eyes, to the touch, to the smell or to the taste.

Everything which appeals to the senses is artistic. There is not only music, painting, sculpture and all the officialy recognized arts, but gastronomy also is an art, as well as perfume making since they appeal to the senses, and above all love is an art.

All art makes use of harmony and therefore enables those who appreciate it to be overrun by something harmonious, which consequently brings in conditions for placing oneself in harmony with infinity.

Literature is particularly important because it contributes to the opening of minds by showing new horizons. Literature for literature's sake is just prattle, what counts is not writing beautiful sentences but the transmitting of new ideas to others by reading.

Audio-visual means are even more important for they appeal to both sight and hearing at the same time. They can replace literature for the better since they are more complete. In the meantime, literature is temporarily useful.

Sensual Meditation

If you want to reach a high level of harmony with infinity, arrange for yourself a place of sensual meditation. Put in it works of art, paintings, reproductions, tapestries, posters, sculptures, drawings, photographs, or anything else designed to represent love, infinity and sensuality, this for the enjoyment of the eyes. Arrange for yourself a corner where you can sit near the ground, on cushions for example, or lie down on a couch or on a fur, this for the pleasure of touch.

Burn pleasant scents, this for the pleasure of the nose. Have a tape recorder on which you will have recorded music that you like, this for the pleasure of the ears. Have trays and bottles filled with food and drink that you like, this for the pleasure of the mouth, and invite one or several people you love according to your tastes, with whom you feel at eas and in harmony, and feed your senses together, ope your bodies so that your minds may open in love an fraternity.

If someone appeals to you physically and if yo feel that it is reciprocal, invite him to this place an together you will be able to reach the sublimatio of harmony which enables you to approach infinity by satisfying your five senses and adding to thi state the synthesis of all these enjoyments, th physical union of two beings in total harmony an

in the illumination of the act of love.

Obviously, harmony must first exist spirituall
That is to say, the minds, and bodies must feel attrac
ed to each other, so that each other's styles corre
pond to each other's tastes. But a spiritual love
always sublimed by a fulfiled physical love. To lov
is to give and expect nothing in exchange. If you lov
somebody, you should give yourself entirely to ther
if they desire it.

You will never be jealous, for jealousy is the oppo
site of love. When one loves somebody, one mus
seek their happiness in all ways and their happines
first of all. To love is to seek the happiness of other
and not your own. If the person you love is attracte
to another, don't be jealous, on the contrary b
happy, if the one you love is happy, even if it's du
to somebody else. Love also the person who want
like you, to bring happiness to the person you love
therefore who has the same goal as you. Jealousy i
the fear that another person may make the one yo
love happier than you can yourself and is the fear o
losing the one you love. On the contrary, we shoul
try to do our best so that the person we love may b
happy, and if somebody else makes them happie
than we do, we should be happy about it becaus
what counts is not that the beloved be happy becaus
of us, but simply that they be happy, regardles
of who makes them happy.

If the being you love is happy with somebody else
rejoice in their happiness.

You will recognize the person who loves you, i

that he will not oppose your happiness with someone else. It is your duty to love the being who loves you that much, by giving them happiness yourself. Therein lies the path of universal love.

Do not reject someone who wants to make you happy, for by accepting them, you make them happy and this is an act of love.

Rejoice in the happiness of others so that they may rejoice in your happiness.

Human Justice

You will not hesitate for one moment between human laws and those of the Creators, because even human judges, will be judged some day by our Creators.

Human laws are indispensable, but they must be improved because they do not take love and fraternity into enough consideration.

The death penalty must be abolished because no man has the right to coldly kill another man in a premeditated and organized manner. Until the time comes when through science, man is able to control the violence which can occur in some people, and cure them of their illness, you will keep criminals apart from society, giving them the love that they lack, while trying to make them understand the monstrosity of their action and giving them the desire to redeem themselves.

Do not mix the big criminals, who are sick from an illness which can be contagious, with people who have committed petty offences, so that they will not be contaminated.

Never forget that all criminals are sick and always consider them as such. We feel scandalised when thinking that once upon a time, we used to suffocate those who had fits of hysteria between two mattresses. We will be just as shocked some day, when we are able to cure and in particular, prevent the sickness of crime, when we look back at how we executed them.

Forgive those who have done you harm without meaning to do so and do not hold a grudge against those who have done you harm willingly. They are ill, for one must be ill to harm one's neighbor. Besides, think how unfortunate are those who harm others, for they will not have the right to eternal life in the gardens of Elohim.

But if someone wants to harm you or those you love, try to subdue him, and if you can't, then, you have the right to defend yourself to save your life or the life of those you love, but never strike with the intention of killing even during legitimate defense, but only to render him harmless, such as knocking him out for example. If the blow you have given turns out to be deadly, without having had the intention to kill, you have nothing to blame yourself for.

You will reduce violent people to impotence by violence, and if necessary by action. Violence is intolerable and you will not tolerate it, even if you have to reduce violent people to impotence by force, but using a non-violent force, that is to say, by a balanced force, and which never acts with the intention of doing harm but of preventing those who do harm from doing it.

Any threat of violence should be considered as severely as a violent action carried out. To threaten to be violent is to think that it is possible to be that way and that this is a way to arrive at one's goals. A person capable of threatening another being with violence is as dangerous as a man who has committed an action of violence, and until we can medically cure those who utter such threats, they must be kept outside of society and we should try to make them understand to what extent their way of behaving is dreadful.

When dealing with the taking of hostages, think first of saving the lives of the innocent who are not in the hands of these sick people and don't give them what they demand. Society must not give those who take hostages what they demand, because by accepting such extortion you will encourage other criminals to do the same and give importance to the threat.

All men should be equal in rights and in power at birth whatever their race is. Do not tolerate racist fools whatever the color of their skin. All the races which populate the earth were created by the Elohim and must be equally respected.

All men on earth must unite to form a world government as it is written in the First Message.

Impose a new world language on all the school children of the entire world. Esperanto exists and if no one propose anything better, choose Esperanto.

Until it becomes possible to abolish money, create a new world currency replacing national currencies. Therein lies the solution to the monetary crisis.

If no one can propose anything better, use the federalist system. Create a federation from the world countries.

Grant independence to those regions who need to be able to organize themselves as they wish. The world will live in harmony if it is no longer composed of separate countries but of regions united in a federation to take charge of earth's destiny.

Science

Science is the most important thing for man. You will keep yourself aware of all the discoveries made by scientists who can solve all problems. Don't let the scientific discoveries fall into the hands of those who think only of getting a profit, nor in the hands of military men who leave some inventions secret in order to retain a hypothetical supremacy on illusory enemies.

Science should be your religion, for the Elohim your Creators created you scientifically. By being scientific, you please your Creators because you act as they do and you show them that you are aware of being made in their image and anxious to exploit all the possibilities that you have.

Science must be used to serve and to liberate mankind, not to destroy and alienate it.

Trust the scientists who are not manipulated by financial interests and trust only these scientists.

You may participate in sports for it is very good for your equilibrium. Particularly those sports that develop self-mastery.

Society should authorize violent and even very violent sports. They are safety valves. An evolved and non-violent society must have violent games which conserve an image of violence enabling the young people who so wish, to be violent with others who wish the same thing and which also allows others to watch these violent exhibitions and release their aggressive vibrations.

You may participate in games which require thought and the use of the mind, but as long as money is not abolished, never play to win money but rather for the pleasure of making your mind function.

You will date your writings counting the year 1946 as the year one after Claude Rael, the last of the prophets. 1976 will therefore be the year 31 after Claude Rael, or the year 31 in the era of Aquarius, or the year 31 of the age of the apocalypse, or the year 31 of the golden age.

The Human Brain

The possibilities of the human brain are far from being entirely known. The sixth sense, direct perception, should be developed in young children. This is what we call telepathy. Telepathy enables us to communicate directly with our Creators, the Elohim.

Numerous mediums have come to me asking me what they should do, because they had received messages from what they call "beyond" asking them to get in touch with me in order to help me and for me to bring them light. Mediums are very important people because they have an above-average gift of telepathy and their brain is on the path to an awakened state. They should make efforts at meditation in order to fully master their possibilities.

I anxiously await all the mediums who have received the order to get in touch with me so that we may organize regular meetings. The true mediums who seek to be informed will all receive instructions.

The power of one brain is great, but the power of several brains is infinite. Let those who have ears, hear.

Never forget that all these things which you don't understand and which your scientists can't explain have been created by the Elohim. The clockmaker knows all the movements of the clock he has made.

The Apocalypse

Do not forget that the apocalypse, that is to say literally the age of revelation, has arrived as has been foreseen.

It is said that when the time comes, there will be many false prophets: you have but to look around you to see that the time has come. False prophets such as horoscope makers, which newspapers are full of, false prophets such as those who keep to every letter of the ancient writings, that is to say, the messages given by the Elohim to the primitive people of ancient times, and who reject the benefits of science. They prefer to believe what narrow minded and primitive people have copied trembling with fear while listening to those whom they considered gods because they came from the sky rather than believing the message transmitted to beings who no longer kneel foolishly before all that which comes from the sky and who try to understand the universe, people to whom we can speak as adults. Look around you and you will see the crowds of fanatic and obscurantist religious sects, which attract young impressionable people thirsty for truth.

A philosopher said: "Jesus came to show the way to follow and men kept their eyes fixed on his finger." Meditate on this sentence. It isn't the messenger who matters but the person who sends the message, and the message itself.

Don't go astray among the oriental sects, the truth is not on the top of the Himalayas any more than in Peru or elsewhere, the truth is in you, but if you want to travel and you like exoticism, go to all these distant countries, and you will understand after you have been there that you have wasted your time and that what you were looking for is in you. Travel inside yourself, otherwise you are but a tourist, a man who passes by and who thinks he will find the truth by watching others searching for it inside themselves. They may find it perhaps but the one watching them won't. And to travel inside yourself, you don't need to take a plane.

The East has nothing to teach the West about wisdom and the awakening of the mind, rather, it is just the opposite. How do you think you will find wisdom among beings who die from hunger while watching herds of "sacred" cows go by? It is on the contrary the West which, with its mind and its science, comes to help people who have been locked up in primitive and murderous beliefs. It is not by chance that the West doesn't face the same problems as the third world countries. Where the mind prevails, the body doesn't die of hunger. Where obscurantism prevails, the body cannot survive. Can primitive people solve the problems of famine in the world and give food to those who are starving? As it is they who are having enough difficulties trying to feed themselves, and you expect to find wisdom there?

All the people of the earth had the same chances at the beginning, some have resolved their problems and even have too much, while others don't even have the means to survive. In your opinion which one can help the other? The people of the West still have a long way to go on the path of open mindedness, but the people of the Orient haven't achieved one-tenth of what the people of the West have achieved.

Telepathic Communication

"Mind and matter are eternally the same thing" (The Tibetan book of the Dead)

If you want to obtain telepathic communications of very high quality, do not cut your hair or your beard. Certain people have a telepathic organ developed enough to work well, even if their head is shaved, but if you want to have the best chances, then, do not cut what the Creators have made grow on your head and face. If it grows, there is a reason, because none of man's physical characteristics were given to him for nothing. By respecting the creation, you respect the Creator.

The best moment to enter into communication with your Creators is on waking, because when your body wakes up, your mind wakes up, too. A mechanism starts up at that point, a mechanism of awakening which you must activate by opening yourself as much as possible to everything around you and to the infinite, being careful not to stop the phenomenon.

Sit down cross-legged, or better still: lie on your back, if possible on the ground and if possible in the open air and look up towards the sky.

The mind is like a rose. In the morning, it begins to open but you always cut it away when it is still just a bud. If you were to wait a little, it will bloom.

To practice physical fitness is good, but to practice the physical fitness of the mind, is better.

And don't be impatient if you don't get any results right away. When an organ is not used, it atrophies. When you have had a plaster for a long time, you need much physical therapy to recover the normal use of the plastered limb.

Look up to the sky and think of the position you

hold in relation to everything which surrounds you, situate yourself in relation to the house which you are in, a tiny spot lost between stone walls, in relation to all the people who are waking up at the same time as you, in relation to those who, in other parts of the globe, are going to bed. Think of all those who are being born, who are uniting with each other physically, who are suffering, who are working or dying as you wake up, and situate yourself in relation to your level accordingly.

Locate yourself too in relation to the infinitely large, think of the town in which you are, a tiny spot lost on a territory which is the country, the continent or the island where you live. Then fly away as if you were in a plane which flies farther and farther away from the ground, until the town is nothing but a tiny spot, then the continent. Be aware of the fact that you are on the earth, a small ball on which humanity is but a parasite, and which spins while you do not even realize that it is spinning, and locate yourself in relation to it and in relation to the moon which revolves around the earth, and in relation to the earth which revolves around the sun, and in relation to the sun also revolving on itself and revolving around the center of our galaxy, and in relation to the stars which are also suns having planets around them on which an infinity of other beings live, among them the planet of our Creators, the Elohim and the planet of the eternals, where you shall one day be admitted for eternity, and in relation to all these worlds where other beings more advanced than us and others more primitive than us live, and in relation to these galaxies which themselves revolve around the center of the universe and locate yourself in relation to our universe, which is itself an atom of a molecule placed perhaps in the arm of a being who is looking up at the sky wondering whether there is life on other planets. This is in relation to the infinitely large.

And situate yourself in relation to your body, to all the organs which make it up and to all the parts which form it, think of all the organs which are working without your noticing, right at this moment, think of your heart which beats without your asking it to, of your blood which circulates and irrigates your whole body, and even your brain, which enables you to reflect and to be conscious of doing so, of all the corpuscles which make up your blood and of all the cells which are in your body being born, which are reproducing while feeling pleasure and which are dying without you knowing it and which perhaps are not conscious that they form the being which you are, and think of all the molecules which constitute these cells, and of the atoms which constitute these molecules and the particles which make up the atoms and which revolve like suns around the center of a galaxy, and of the particles of the particles on which beings live and ask themselves if there is life on other planets. This in relation to the infinitely small.

Be in harmony with the infinitely large and with the infinitely small by giving love towards above and towards below and by being conscious that you yourself are part of infinity.

Then try to transmit by intensely thinking your message of love to the Elohim, our Creators, transmitting to them your wish to see them and to be among them one day and to have the strength of deserving to be among the chosen.

Then you will feel light and ready to do good around you with all your strength all day long, because you will be in harmony with infinity.

You may also do these exercises in the sensual meditation room, during the day, alone or with other persons.

But the moment when you approach closest to the perfect harmony with infinity, is when this takes place in your room of sensual meditation with a being you love and by physically uniting with him, placing yourselves both together in harmony with infinity during your union.

In the evening, when the sky is full of stars and the temperature is mild, lie down on the ground, behold the stars while thinking intensely of the Elohim and wishing that you may deserve to be some day among them and thinking strongly that you are available and ready to do exactly what they may ask of you, even if you don't understand very well why they are asking it of you. You will perhaps see a signal if you are sufficiently ready.

When you are lying there, on your back, realize to what extent your organs of perception are limited which explains the difficulties you may have in conceiving infinity. A force keeps you nailed to the ground and you cannot with a jerk fly away to the

stars, yet you don't see any rope holding you down, millions of people are listening to thousands of radio stations and are watching hundreds of television programs which are broadcast in the atmosphere, and yet you don't see these waves and you don't hear them, and compasses have all their pointers drawn to the north and yet you neither see nor hear the forces which draw them. There I repeat to you, your organs of perception are very limited and energies like the universe are infinite. Wake up and awaken the organs you have in you and which enable you to pick up the waves which you can't pick up or don't even suspect the existence of. Simple pigeons are able to find the north and you, a human, wouldn't be able to? Think for a moment.

And teach your children, whose organs are developing, all this, this is how the new Man will be born, whose faculties will be infinitely superior to those of present man.

When his growth is finished, a man who never learned to walk will always be a cripple, and even if he is taught later, he will always be handicapped even if he is very gifted.

It is during their growth that you must open your children's minds so that all their faculties may blossom, and they will be new men, who will have nothing in common with what we are: poor, narrow minded primitives.

The Reward

Let this book guide those who recognize and love our Creators, the Elohim.

Who believe in them and don't forget to communicate telepathically with them, rediscovering the original meaning of prayer, and who do good to their fellow men.

Who believe in what was revealed to me and in what was revealed before me, and who are sure that scientific reincarnation is a reality.

Those people have a guide and an aim in life and they are happy.

As for those who aren't awakened, it is useless to speak to them about this message, a being who is asleep can't hear and the unconscious mind does not wake up in just a few instants, particularly if the one who is sleeping finds his sleep very comfortable.

But spread this message around you to those who do good to other men, and particularly among those who by using the brain which the Elohim gave them, relieve men of fear of the shortage of food, diseases, and daily efforts by giving them the time to fulfil themselves and blossom. For them are reserved the gardens of the planet of the eternals and their thousand fountains.

For it isn't enough not to do any harm to others without doing them good. A being whose life has been neutral will be entitled to neutrality, that is to say he will not be recreated, neither to pay for his crimes since he does not commit any, nor to receive the reward of his good deeds since he doesn't perform any.

Someone who has made many people suffer during part of his life, and then makes up for it by doing as much good as he did harm will also be neutral.

To have the right to scientific reincarnation on the planet of the eternals, one must have at the end of one's life a distinctly positive appraisal.

To be satisfied with doing good on a small scale around oneself is enough for someone who is not of superior intelligence or who has no means, but it is not enough for someone who is very intelligent or who is wealthy. A very intelligent being has the duty to use the mind given to him by the Elohim to bring happiness to other men by inventing new techniques improving their living conditions.

And those who will be entitled to scientific reincarnation on the planet of the Elohim will live eternally in a world where food will be brought to them without them having to make the slightest effort, and where marvellously beautiful female and male partners scientifically created for this purpose, will be there only to satisfy their pleasures, and they will live there eternally, seeking only to fulfil themselves doing what they please.

As for those who made others suffer, they will be recreated and their suffering will be equal to the pleasure of the eternals.

How can you not believe in all this now that science and ancient religions are coming together perfectly.

You were nothing but matter, dust, and the Elohim made you living beings able to dominate matter, in their image, and you will again become matter, dust, and they will make you live again, as they have created you, scientifically.

The Elohim created the first men without knowing that they were doing what had already been done for them, they thought they were only doing a scientific experiment without great interest, and that is why the first time they destroyed almost all humanity, but when they understood that they had been created like us, they begain to love us as their own children and swore never to try to destroy us, leaving us to overcome our own violence by ourselves.

The Elohim, although they do not directly intervene in favor or against humanity as a whole, they do however, act on some individuals whose actions please or displease them. Woe to those claiming to have met them or to have received a message from them if it is not true, their life will become a hell and they will regret their lie when facing all the troubles they will have.

And those who act against the Guide of Guides and try to keep him from carrying out his mission or who go along with him in order to spread strife among those who follow him will also see their life become a hell and they will know why, without anything seeming to be due to an influence coming from above, diseases, family, professional and sentimental worries and other things will invade their earthly existence while waiting for the eternal punishment.

You who smile while reading these lines, you are among those who would have crucified Jesus if you had lived at that time, yet now you want to see your families be born, get married and die under his effigy because this has become part of our morals and customs.

And you cast ironic smiles on those who believe in these writings saying that they should spend some time in a psychiatric asylum and you behave like those who went to see the lions eating the first Christians, for now, when someone has disturbing ideas he is no longer crucified nor given as food to wild beasts, this is far too barbaric, but rather he is sent to a psychiatric asylum. Had these establishments existed two thousand years ago, Jesus and those who believed in him would had been confined to them.

As for those who believe in eternal life, ask them why they shed tears when they lose a beloved one.

As long as man was unable to scientifically understand the Elohim's work, it was natural for man to believe in an impalpable god, but now that by science, man understands matter, the infinitely large and the infinitely small, he no longer has the right to believe in the god his primitive ancestors believed in. The Elohim, our Creators, intend to be recognized by those who are now capable of understanding how life can be created and of making a comparison with the ancient writings. Those people will have the right to eternity.

And you, Christian, you have read a hundred times that Jesus would return, and if he came back you would put him in a psychiatric asylum. Come, open your eyes!

And you, son of Israel, you are still waiting for your messiah and you don't open your door!

And you, Buddhist, your writings indicate that the new Buddha will be born in the West, recognize the anticipated signs!

And you, Muslim, Muhammad reminded you that the Jews had made an error when they killed the prophets, and that the Christians had also made an error in adoring the prophet more than the one who sent the prophet, welcome the last of the prophets and love those who sent him!

If you recognize the Elohim as your Creators, if you love them and wish to welcome them, if you try to do good to other people by making as much use as possible of all your possibilities, if you think of your Creators regularly, trying through telepathy to make them understand you love them, if you help the Guide of Guides to accomplish his mission, you will without a doubt be entitled to scientific reincarnation on the planet of the eternals.

When man discovered the energies required to get him to the moon, he also found sufficient energies to destroy all life on earth.

"The hour has drawn near, and the moon is rent asunder." (The Koran, Sura 54, verse 1)

Any day now, man can self-destroy himself. Only those who follow the last of the prophets will be saved from destruction.

In former times, Noah was not believed and

people laughed at him when he was preparing for the destruction. But they were not the last ones to laugh.

And when the Elohim told the inhabitants of Sodom and Gomorrah to leave the town without looking back, some didn't believe what was announced and were destroyed.

Now we have come to the time when man himself may destroy all life on earth, and only those who recognize the Elohim as their Creators will be saved from destruction. You may still not believe any of this, but when the time comes you will think of these lines again, but it will be too late.

And when the cataclysm takes place, for there is a good chance that it will happen and quite soon too, given the way men are presently behaving, there will be two sorts of men, those who haven't recognized their Creators and have not followed the last of the prophets, and those who opened their ears and their eyes and recognized what had been announced a long time ago.

The former will undergo the sufferings of destruction in the final furnace and the others will be spared and taken with the Guide of Guides to the planet of the eternals where they will enjoy a marvellous life of fulfilment, blossoming and pleasure with the ancient wise men. They will be served by magnificent athletes with sculptural bodies who will bring them refined food which they will savor in the company of men and women of unequaled beauty and charm and entirely submitted to their desires.

"Seated on couches inwrought with gold and jewels,
Reclining thereon facing each other,
There will wait on them youths, who will not age,
Carrying goblets and ewers and cups filled out of a flowing spring,
No headache will they get there from, nor will they be intoxicated,
And carrying such fruits as they choose,
And flesh of birds as they may desire,
And there will be fair maidens with wide,
Lovely eyes,
Like pearls, we preserved,
As a reward for what they did."
(The Koran, Sura 56, verses 16 to 25)

You who believe in all that is written here, when the Guide of Guides summons you somewhere, drop everything, for it might be because he has received some information concerning the end. And if you are near him at that moment, you will be saved and taken with him, far from the sufferings.

You who believe, don't pass judgement on the actions or words of the Elohim. The created does not have the right to judge its Creator. Respect our prophet and don't pass judgement on his actions and his words, for we hear through his ears, we see through his eyes and we speak through his mouth. By lacking respect towards the prophet, you lack respect towards those who sent him, towards your Creators.

The messages which have been given by the Elohim, and the people who adhered fully were in the truth, but it was the obscurantist systems which were built on these messages and which used those who had a feeling for the messages, which were in the wrong. The Church is vanishing and it deserves just that. As for the men of the church, let those who have their eyes open join the last of the prophets and help him spread the messages which were handed to him, throughout the world. He will welcome them with open arms and they will be able to blossom and fulfil themselves fully while being the messengers of those whom they had always believed in but this time finally understanding truly what their work was when they created men and when they sent Jesus.

With him, they will really be able to fulfil themselves,. free from the restraints of the Church which is fossilised and encrusted by thousands of years' deposits of crimes and criminal inquisitions. They will be able to do what they should do, that is to say use their organs their Creators gave them, for the Creators do not like you not using the organs they gave you. They will be able to enjoy their five senses and unite physically for ever or for an instant of happiness with whom they like without feeling guilty, on the contrary, it is now that they should feel guilty, guilty of not using all that was given to them by the Creators.

And they will truly be openers of minds instead of being those who put people to sleep.

Already, there are almost no more seminarists, but some people are unhappy, those who feel in themselves the vocation to bring love around them and open minds. Fifty years ago, there were fifty thousand seminarists, now there are only five hundred, this means that there are at least forty nine thousand five hundred who are unhappy, those who have in them the potential for radiating truth and harmony placed by our Creators for them to use. But they do not feel attracted by this church covered with crimes and obscurity.

You who are among these forty nine thousand five hundred, and feel the need to radiate and do something for your fellow men, you who want to remain faithful to your Creators and to Jesus when he told you to love one another and to respect The Creators, "The Father who is in heaven", you who feel that this message is true, come with us and become Guides, that is to say people who devote themselves to the Elohim, in the tradition of Moses, Elijah and Jesus, and to the spreading of their messages while living a normal life, in other words truly fulfiling yourselves and enjoying all the senses which your Creators gave you.

You who are presently members of the church, take off those clothes which are as sad as their colours, the colours of the crimes which have been committed under their facade. Come with us and become guides for mankind on the path of universal peace and universal love.

Leave those Churches which are nothing but monuments raised by primitives, temples where they could adore valueless things, pieces of wood and pieces of metal. The Elohim have no need for temples in every city in order to feel loved, all they require is that men try to communicate through telepathy with them, thus rediscovering the original meaning of prayer, by opening themselves to infinity and not by shutting themselves away in obscure and mystical stone buildings.

Hypocrisy and mystification have lasted long enough. On the basis of true messages, organizations were built which fattened themselves on these messages, living in misplaced luxury and using people's fear to reach their ends. Wars were waged under the pretext of diffusing these messages. Shame!

The money of the poor has been used to build a financial power. Shame!

Love of one's neighbor has been preached with weapons in hand. Shame!

Equality of men has been preached while supporting dictatorships. Shame!

It was said "god is with us", as a good way of launching men to fratricidal wars. Shame!

The gospels have been read and reread which said: "And you will make no man call you father upon the earth: for you have only one Father, he who is in heaven." (Matthew 23:9*) and yet they have repeatedly made themselves be called my father and my lord. Shame!

Texts have been read and reread which said: "Do not take along any gold, nor silver nor brass in your purses. Take no bag for your journey, nor even a

*added in translation

spare pair of shoes, coat nor yet staves." (Matthew 10:9,10*) And yet they have wallowed in the luxury of the Vatican. Shame!

The pope, if he does not sell all the properties of the Vatican to help the unfortunate, will not be admitted among the righteous on the planet of the eternals, for it is shameful to wallow in a luxury acquired at the expense of poor people by using true messages and by exploiting births, unions and the deaths of men.

But if all this changes, and if the people who were a part of this monstrous organization without understanding their mistake, leave it and regret their error, they will be forgiven and entitled to eternity, for the Elohim, our Creators, love us, their children, and forgive those who sincerely regret their errors.

The church has no reason to exist any longer, for it was entrusted with the spreading of the message of Jesus in anticipation of the age of apocalypse, and this age has come, and the church has used methods of dissemination which are a shame to them.

Although it has accomplished its mission, it will be reproached with all its crimes and those who still wear its clothes full of blood will be among the guilty. Wake up, sleeper that you are! All this is no story. Reread all the writings of the ancient prophets, become informed about the most recent scientific discoveries, especially in biology, and look at the sky. The announced signs are there! The unidentified

*added in translation

flying objects, which man has called "flying saucers" appear every day. "There will be signs in the sky" that has been written a long time ago. . . .

Once you have informed yourself of these things, make a synthesis, and wake up, Claude Rael exists, he is indeed alive, he did not write what Moses, Ezekiel, Elijah, Jesus, Muhammad, Buddha and all others wrote, he is not a biologist, but he is the last of the line of prophets, the prophet of the Apocalypse, that is to say of the time when everything can be understood. He is living right now near you, and you are lucky enough to be one of his contemporaries and to receive his teaching, wake up, pull yourself together and take to the road, go to see him and help him, he needs you! You will be one of the pioneers of the final religion, the religion of religions, and you will have your place, whatever may happen, among the righteous for eternity, savoring the delights of the planet of the eternals, in the company of marvellously pleasant beings submitted to your desires.

The Guides

You will follow the Guide of Guides, for he is the ambassador of the Elohim, our Creators, our fathers who are in heaven.

You will follow all the advice given in this book because it is the advice of your Creators, transmitted by the mouth of Claude Rael, our ambassador, the last of the prophets, the shepherd of shepherds, and you will help him to build the religion of religions.

Jew, Christian, Muslim, Buddhist and you who have another religion, open your eyes and ears, reread your holy writings and you will understand that this book is the last one, the one announced by your own prophets, and come with us to prepare the coming of our Creators, write to the Guide of Guides and he will put you in contact with other people who, like you, are Raelians, that is to say believe in the messages transmitted by Claude Rael, and he will put you in contact with a guide in your region so that you may meet regularly to meditate and in order that you may act to spread this message so that it be known all over the world.

You who are reading this message, be aware that you are privileged and think of all those who do not know about it yet, do all you can to make sure that no one around you is ignorant of these fantastic revelations without ever trying to convince those to whom you speak about it. Bring these messages to their knowledge and if they are ready they will open by themselves. Always repeat to yourself this sentence of Gandhi, "it is not because no one sees the truth that it becomes an error".

You who feel so exhilarated in reading these messages and who wish to radiate this truth and make it shine around you, you who want to live by devoting yourself totally to our Creators by applying scrupulously what they ask, by trying to guide men on the path of fulfilment and blossoming, you should become a Guide if you want to be fully capable of this. Write to the Guide of Guides, to Claude Rael, he will welcome you and will have you go through an initiation enabling you to radiate fully, for one can open the minds of others only if one's own mind is open.

The love of the Creators for their work is immense, and you should return them this love, you should love them as they love you and prove it to them by helping their ambassador and those who help him and by putting all your means and all your strength at their service so that they may really build an embassy to welcome them and travel around the world to make the message radiate.

If you wish to help me realize the aims set by the Elohim, write to me:

Claude Raël
International Raelian Movement
Case postale 225
CH-1211, Geneva 8, Switzerland

And don't forget the regular meetings, the reunions of people who believe in the messages, every year, on the first Sunday of April, August 6th, October 7th and December 13th. The site of the meeting will be indicated in the liaison bulletin, by the Raelian Movement of your country. (Address listed in the back pages)

Location of Puy-De-La-Sola,
place of the first encounter, and of
ROC PLAT, place of the second encounter.

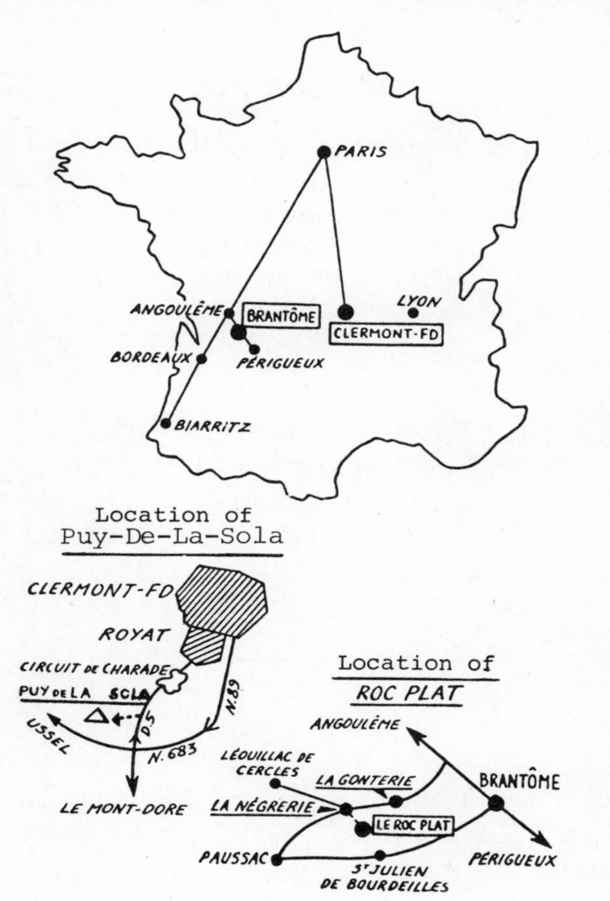

BIBLIOGRAPHY

THE BARDO THODOL

Tibetan Book of the Dead
Re-published in 1974 at the
Librairie d'Amérique et d'Orient
Edition Maisonneuve
11, rue Saint-Sulpice
PARIS

Other books written by Rael
"Let's Welcome Oùr Fathers From Space"
"Geniocracy"
"Sensual Meditation"

In order to recognize one another among believers, wear the medal decorated with the symbol of infinity which is the emblem of our Creators, moreover, it functions as a psychic catalyst during the attempts of telepathic communication with the Elohim and contributes to the awakening of mind.

If you wish to have one of these medals, write to the Raelian Movement of your country (addresses listed in back pages) or write to the office responsible for your continent.

How To Contact The Raelian Movement

1. Write to or call The Raelian Movement of your country if the address is listed in the back pages of this book.
   They will answer your questions and send you:
   a) Information on local meetings and activities, etc.
   b) An Application Form for Admission To The Raelian Movement of your country.
   c) Information on Cellular Transmission

2. If you do not find The Raelian Movement of your country in the list, write to:
   a) If you live in Europe:
   Mouvement Raelien International
   Case Postale 225
   CH-1211, Genève 8
   Suisse
   b) If you live in the Americas:
   Canadian Raelian Movement
   P.O. Box 86
   Youville Station
   Montreal, Quebec
   Canada H2P 2V2   Phone: 1-514-681-6263
   c) If you live in Africa:
   Mouvement Raelien Africain
   INJS
   BP V 54 Abidjan
   Côté d' Ivoire

d) If you live in Asia and Oceania:
Japanese Raelian Movement
P.O. Box 15 Shitaya-Station
Taito-ku, Tokyo
Japan 110-91

FAX: Country Code 81, City Code 3, 844-7109
81-3-844-7109
Phone: 81-3-842-4129

How To Attend Raelian Seminar to be held every year

Seminar in France: 2 weeks starting August 6.
(you may attend 1 week only)
Seminar in Canada: 2 weeks during the last two weeks in July.
(you may attend 1 week only)
Seminar in Japan: 1 week during the 1st week in May
(you may attend 4 days only)

For application form, write to French/Canadian/Japanese Raelian Movement respectively.

*International Raelian Movement
Case postale 225
CH-1211, Geneva 8
Switzerland

EUROPE

Mouvement Raelien Suisse
Case postale 225
CH-1211, Genève 8
Suisse

Mouvement Raelien Français
BP 26
75660 Paris Cédex 14
France

Mouvement Raelien Belge
52, Rue Rys de Mosbeux
B-4940 Trooz
Belgique

British Raelian Mouvement
BCM Minstrel
London WC1N 3XX
Great Britain

Movimento Raeliano Italiano
CP 13/173
I-00185 Roma 4 Terme
Italy

Movimiento Raeliano Espanol
Miguel-Angel Peinado
Bernado Lopez Garcia 11
E-Madrid
Spain

German Raelian Movement
(Deutsche Rael-Bewegung)
Postfach 1502
D 8450 Amberg
F.R. Germany

Austrian Raelian Movement
Postfach 146
2340 Mödling
Austria

AFRICA

Movement Raelian Congolais
27, rue Père Dréan
Bacongo
Brazzaville, Congo

Mouvement Raelien du Burkina Faso
B.P. 8224
Ouagadougou
Burkina Faso

*CanadianRaelian Movement
P.O. Box 86
Youville Station
Montreal, Quebec
Canada H2P PV2 Phone: 1-514-681-6263

Movimiento Raelien Mexicano
Apartado Postal 57-002
06500, D.F.
Mexico

Mouvement Raelien Haitien
a/s Mouvement Raelien Canadien
CP 86 Station Youville
Montreal Quebec
Canada H2P 2V2

Mouvement Raelien Guadeloupéen
B.P. 3105 Raizet-Sud
971 Abymes
Guadeloupe

Mouvement Raelien Martinique
B.P. 60001
Fort de France
Martinique

*Japanese Raelian Movement
P.O. Box 15
Shitaya Station
Taito-ku
Tokyo, Japan 110-91
Fax: 81-3-844-7109
Phone: 81-3-842-4129

Korean Raelian Movement
c/o K.S. Bae
K.P.O. Box 399
Seoul, Korea

Taiwan Raelian Movement
P.O. Box 7-0692
Taipei, Taiwan, Republic of China
Fax: 886-2-782-0080

Thai Raelian Movement
10/3 Soi Taweechertchu
Huay-Khwang
Bangkok 10400
Thailand

* offices responsible for the continent/region

☐ Please send me information on Raelian Movement
☐ I wish to join The Raelian Movement. Please mail an application form to me.

Name ______________________

Address ______________________

City ____________ State ____________ Post Code ____________

Country ______________________

Message:

____

____

____

____

____

Mail above coupon to Raelian Movement near you.